Ee-ore's

VOLUME I

LEONARD VEDDER

authorHOUSE®

AuthorHouse™
1663 Liberty Drive
Bloomington, IN 47403
www.authorhouse.com
Phone: 1-800-839-8640

Published by AuthorHouse   07/25/2012

ISBN: 978-1-4772-1337-7 (sc)
ISBN: 978-1-4772-1338-4 (e)

Library of Congress Control Number: 2012910019

EE·ORE'S
LIBERTY RAG

A FREE PRESS, IMPLEMENTING FLEXIBLE POLICIES
AND FLEXIBLE PRINTING SCHEDULES ALL FLEXABLY
PUBLISHER . . . . . . I. TROLL
EDITOR . . . . . . TWINK
ASSISTANT EDITOR . . . . EE-ORE
GOPHER & FLUNKIE . . . LEONARD VEDDER
ADDRESS RT. 2, BOX 570, BANDON, OREGON 97411

Dedicated to LIBERTY'S PRESERVANCY
As opposed to Nature Conservancy
    Published by Troll Enterprises
Located under the Bear Creek Bridge

YESTER RANT

LIBERTY RAG

===

A FREE PRESS, IMPLEMENTING
FLEXIBLE POLICIES

AND FLEXIBLE PRINTING
SCHEDULES ALL FLEXIBLY

PUBLISHER . . . . . . I. TROLL

EDITOR . . . . . . TWINK

ASSISTANT . . . . EE-ORE
EDITOR

GOPHER & . . . LEONARD
FLUNKIE VEDDER

ADDRESS RT. 2 BOX 570, BANDON,
OREGON 97411

Dedicated to
LIBERTY'S
PRESERVANCY
As opposed to Nature
Conservancy Published
by Troll Enterprises
Located under the Bear
Creek Bridge

INTRODUCTION

All species have ever been jeopardized by nature's constant demand for each species adaption to an ever changing habitat. Species now extinct are those that failed to adequately adapt to earth's constant change, and their numbers far exceed those of species that survive today.

The only means for any specie to gain sustenance is that of exploiting other species, both past and present. Many species, if not all, even exploit their own through competition for survival. Often the exploitation is referred to as a food chair, but it is generally not linear, having many branches instead.

Some might argue that some species exist which sustain themselves on chemicals or chemical compounds, failing to recognize that much of earth's surface is made up of chemical residue from species of the past. A mere graveyard of those species that went before.

The common consensus today has it that the species of mankind became civilized when he undertook agriculture, domesticating exploitable species for his sustenance. In effect, species man domesticated himself at one and the same time, because he could then forego the transient lifestyle of the hunter-gatherer.

Since becoming civilized, man has learned through propagation and selective breeding to enhance desirable characteristics in exploitable domesticated species. He has further learned to crossbreed and to artificially produce hybrids for the same reasons.

The timeworn theory that there is no action that does not cause reaction here applies. Man has learned that causing a Specie To attain desirable traits, Often has a desultory effect with the species losing losing other desirable traits. Common desirable breeds of domesticated animals often harbor regressive traits, and domesticated plant species share the same hazard.

When a domesticated specie is perceived as so superior to other types, that it alone is bred or cultivated, then that specie, having single genetic uniformity, is at risk to single adverse natural forces. Consequently, scientists college and preserve seeds of less desirable types as to maintain genetic diversity within mankinds supply. Efforts in animal husbandry seek to attain similar goals.

Earth's human population; 8,000 BC, 4 million agriculture begins

1,830	1 billion
1930	2 billion
1960	3 billion
1975	4 billion
1993	5½ billion

At the current population growth rate of 1.7 percent, earth's population will reach 700 trillion prior to the year 2700.

Certainly the preservation of species that mankind can exploit for his practical use, should be given the highest priority. Even with the technical knowledge which man possesses, man may well prove sorely lacking for overcoming nature's way in his quest for survival. The preservation of species for theoretical idealistic or speculative reasons, is an effort that mankind can ill afford to undertake. That our government has been steered to such a course of folly is a situation that must be quickly terminated.

We cannot continue to allow governmental handouts to apolitical "non-profit" preservationist organizations, who then use the funds accrued to further the folly with their lobby. The folly that has seen the Federal Resource agencies, Bureau of Land Management and the United States Forest Service publicly proclaim that they are changing planned management to emphasize ECOSYSTEM. ECOSYSTEM being a term which lacks any valid definition, these agencies plan to emphasize the unknown! Interior Secretary Babbitt has been quoted as offering, "an ECOSYSTEM IS IN THE EYE OF THE BEHOLDER". That certainly accomplished little in raising the term from the murky realm of the undefined.

Quoting Julian Huxley from THE BIOLOGIST LOOKS AT MAN, "Sociologists are beginning to realize that existing ethic or religious systems often contain a large element of psychological compensation: they compensate for the miseries of this world with the bliss of a world to come, they compensate for ignorance of fact with certitude of feeling, they compensate for actual imperfections of ethical practice by setting up impossible ethical ideals. This is not merely hypocrisy, it is a primitive method of self defense against a hard and difficult reality".

The magnitude of the specie preservation issue demands a rapid resolution on clearly defined lines of what is, and what is not, practical for mankind and his future generations.

Again quoting Huxley, but now addressing mans rightful place: "The supernatural is in part the region of the natural that has not yet been understood, in part an invention of human fantasy, In part the unknowable. Body and soul are not separate entities but two aspects of one organization, and man is that portion of the universal world stuff that has evolved until it is capable of rational and purposeful values. His place in the universe is to continue that evolution and to realize those values".

Most of our lawmakers have been overwhelmed by the deluge of folly forwarded by the preservationist lobby, funded in part by our own tax money which the preservationists acquire from the Interior Department agencies for "helping" in the land acquisition process. Consequently lawmakers forward the folly of preserving species for impractical reasons by vast spending for specie set asides and implementing countless rules that regulate the activities of man so as to bar him from his rightful place.

In his HISTORY OF THE PELOPONNESIAN WAR, Thucydides quoted his political rival Pericles, "We all look with distaste on those people who arrogantly pretend to a reputation of which they are not entitled; we should equally condemn those who, through lack of moral fibre, fail to live up to the reputation which is theirs already".

Many of our elected and appointed leaders have, in effect, condemned themselves by their own actions. None the less, a speedy removal from office should be vested upon each that endeavored to forward folly, for their demonstrated lack of integrity in guarding our basic human liberties.

ECO' CRITIQUE

The homeless increase, week by week !
Soon, we'll be farmless, so to speak,
With farms usurped by eco' freak,
For specie set asides, they seek.

Without the foods the farmers eke,
Man will become a hungry geek,
And thirsty too, if he's so meek,
To yield the rivers, ponds and creek'.

Should legislators, tongue in cheek,
Allow the plan that eco's wreak,
The earth will then become unique,
A realm for feather, fang and beak !

Vexing Verse of Vedder

THE AWESOME PREDATOR

Our present day calamity
Began in nineteen seventy
When Rockefeller hatched the plot
How private property be got
To "save" endangered plant and beast
An effort now greatly increased
By the Endangered species Act
Excluding man, and that's a fact.

Now many government agencies
Are plotting day and night to seize
The titles of the landed folk
By any hook or crook or stroke.

Agencies of Fish and Wildlife
Cause title holders naught but strife
And seek their land for this or that
Endangered species habitat,
And agencies, we understand
That do manage the Federal land
Now have a program, where they flirt
With usurping of private dirt.

While many others covet yet
Of any ground that may be wet
To point where they would put their stamp
On any ground which one was damp.

And water boards commence the fight
To deny those with water right',
For all the water, they would glom
To save some speckled diatom.

'Mong those impacted by this move
Are farmers seeking to improve
The methods in which they are able
To provide mankind with his table
And they need wet and dirt to grow
Those edibles from seeds they sow
'Cause burgers, beans and 'tater starches
Don't grow beneath McDonald arches.

It's from some soil tillers lot
That all those tasty things are got!

So, to those Eco' Activist'
Who arrogantly would insist
That Mother Earth return in time
To stages they might deem sublime.
We'd point out that there was an age
On Earth, when only fires rage'
And other times, it wasn't nice
Because of all the snow and ice
And surely there was once a time
When only living thing was slime.

So, when you list your prioritys
For beasts and birds and plants and trees
We adamantly would insist
Mankind's included on your list
And that he's left with role complete
With time and space, so to compete
And not denied his rightful chance
For earning of his sustenance.

Because you're seeking to restore
The Earth to some stage gone before,
We recognize and we deplore
You as man's AWESOME PREDATOR!

LOGIPHOBICS

Beware logic driven by fear,
In propaganda that we hear,
Which often is contrived to blear,
The fact it's premise is not near,
To any truth that we'd hold dear,
But has been so designed, to steer,
By means of false premise, unclear,
A logic forwarded, quite queer,
Of false conclusions that appear.

FALSEHOODS AND FACTORED FEAR

An oft' repeated lie has some,
Merit providing momentum,
For propaganda fed to us.

Moreso if truth, especially,
Is clouded in obscurity,
To provide greater impetus.

thus, propaganda starts by way,
Of oft' repeated lies they'd lay,
Where truth remains intangible,

As a means to set in motion,
Propaganda, they've a notion,
To profit by feeding us full.

Once propaganda is started,
Factored fear is then imparted,
As means to gain a driving force.

For factored fear clouds the issue,
By keeping the full truth from view,
Thus, propaganda stays the course.

So when we're fed, repeatedly,
Statements with ambiguity,
Of truth in matters concerning,

It's then we'd better question why,
Such repetitions they'd apply,
Other than deny discerning.

And better if we recognize,
Our need to fully analyze,
Issues driven by factored fear,

Testing to see if it's mere spawn,
Derived from false conclusion drawn,
Which some truthless premise would steer.

NOMINEE FOR DUBIOUS AWARDS

Evidence from earlier age,
Indicates that ODOT was sage,
    Enough to straighten out a curve,
    As rules of common sense observe.
For we know that a road where bent,
Is predisposed for accident.
    Now from that policy, they stray,
    Off another tangental way,
Due to such planning, they insist,
We gain curves that did not exist.
    Before, to "wisdom, infinite",
    At building curves, they did commit !
At forty two and one oh one,
The recently rebuilt j unction,
    We now have curve, where there was none,
    Before construction had begun.
Drivers from Bandon going east,
Must now negotiate curve least,
    Distance from the intersection,
    As they look in back direction,
Because with traffic, they must merge,
From intersection that converge'.
    Saddest of all, it is to say,
    They could have left the straightaway,
There's room enough where old road lay,
Instead of merging curve which they,
    All east bound drivers do betray,
To accidents along the way !
With accidents the consequence,
ODOT should have the common sense,
    To not display incompetence,
    With monumental negligence !
All apt conclusions surely say,
It's best to merge on straightaway,
    With intersections far away,
    Because that is the safest way !

AROINT!

When little Willie smoked a joint,
"Did not inhale", he made point.

When Will found internes to anoint,
He said, "Such was not sex, conjoint",
In testimony, he'd appoint,
With perjuries that disappoint.

Demos marched to his counterpoint,
Which rendered congress so disjoint',
They could not demand Will aroint.

Thus, demos served to disappoint,
Our justice system's major point.

Come ballot time, folks can appoint,
A means to tell demos, "Aroint !"

NASTY NUGGETS

It's sure that once upon a time,
The meat of chicken was thought prime,
For then, 'twould been considered crime,

If those who drew the entrails out,
Spread chicken poopy all about,
The chicken carcass, there's no doubt!

Today, chicken entrails are spat,
By a machine which does just that,
Then dumps carcasses in a vat,

Which mixes poopy in a brew,
Permeating the meat through and through,
Before it's sold to me and you.

Processors claim this perfidy,
Is mere advanced technology,
That they not foist on you and me,

With consumers prone to defer,
Any statement which might aver,
It's black or white they most prefer.

THE BRILLIG WABE

Pray tell, what is the cause of late,
That common postage, first class rate,
Has fees that ever escalate?

The P.O. seems to think it wise,
If the junk rates, they subsidize,
By causing first class rates to rise,

To point where it will compensate,
And subsequently pay the freight,
For mail with a junkish trait.

That junk which does not advertise,
Comes in such varied shape and size,
Expeditious sort, it denies !

Junk mail fees should full equate,
To extra junk sort time they slate,
With charges full commensurate !

Instead, first class rates climb higher,
By the P.O.s logic, wryer,
Than slivey tove's gimbel, gyre !

John Q. Public
Main Street
U. S. A.

Dear John,
Wake up John Q. Public, wipe your eyes from the blear,
Before we've lost liberties, that long we've held dear,
For a covetous dragon has lately appear',
Who's seeking for folk liberty, naught but a bier.
    Dragon's bedded with government, to engineer,
    Vast restrictions, that with liberty interfere,
    And with takings of properties, year after year,
    As preserves for species, all 'cross our hemisphere.
Yet providing for species all skittles and beer,
At cost of folk liberties, dragon would shear,
All properties taken by this land bucaneer,
Leaves naught for John Q. Public but circumstance' drear.
    Now functioning as Interior charioteer,
    And perceived profiting "non-profit" profiteer,
    The dragon is taking properties we revere,
    And seeks non-disclosure so his tracks disappear.
This creed crowing dragon likens to chanticleer,
And his creed, he'd sustain with a science quite queer,
Dragon's 'logical'" has no logic near,
So he'd broach the scenarios, public does fear.
    Now John, we'd hope that you'd become mutineer,
    In mutiny where vox populi persevere,
    And duel with this dragon that now domineer',
    Regaining for liberty a life less severe.
So take up the gauntlet, dragon's cast on our sphere,
And full smite the dragon with a smash in his sneer,
While guarding yourself, that the dragon not sear,
All the remnants of liberty left in the rear.
    And should you gain end to the dragon's career,
    'Twill be said, in the future that you had adhere',
    To freedom and liberty, that they not be spear',
    By the dragon and all that the dragon has smear'.
For should be regain helm, ship of state you might steer,

To latitudes promising weather more clear,
Then likely you'll merit, from your crew a cheer,
For having cast off from preservationist pier.
    Because when you have steered from that folly so sheer,
    And wiped from libert's eyes, all of the tear',
    You will gain many laurels from all sonneteer',
    I yet am remaining, your truly, sincere.

                                        Fearfor Suchdrear

P.S. I sure failed to mention, when I had your ear,
    A few things that you likely would leave not hear
    That dragon has got to be gotten from here,
    So if you please, GET YOUR TAIL INTO GEAR !

DRAGON DROPPINGS !

There's certainly no mystery,
Within our country's history,
It's founding based on liberty,
Bequeathed to us in legacy,
From founders seeking to be free.

Today, Self claimed ecologist',
And pseudo-sci biologist
Join with preservationist',
And green environmentalist',
To seek our liberties desist.

As we perceive their master plan,
For saving species, in the van,
Of species all, excepting man.
For man restrictions that would ban,
The liberties of human clan.

So we have green dragon profound,
Seeking preserves that all abound,
Excepting man, whom thet'd surround,
With 'stricted liberties compound',
By usurping man's private ground.

"Non-profit" dragon, while tax free,
Has gained Interior subsidy,
Of funding taxed from you and me,
By helping usurp property,
While denying our liberty'.

Thus, dragon is quite opulent,
Can lobby laws that document,
All dragon plot requirement',
For liberties in banishment,
For each and every resident.

So, woe to man, lest he perceive,
What dragon has hid up his sleeve,
And demand government now cleave,
The dragon from the web he'd weave,
And seek our liberties reprieve !

DEAR INTERAGENCY SEIS TEAM

My greetings, team SEIS,
I'd like to comment and express,
My views how Option Nine transgress',
Right' liberty which man is bless'.
   Nine fosters economic mess,
   For all who dwell in the northwes',
   And by extension, more than less'
   The nation's 'conomy is stress'.
Nine further fails to address,
The needs of folk, who'd homes possess,
With timber products priced excess'
From want of that resource access.
   Nine also causes much distress,
   With heinie-wipes in full supress',
   'Cause cobs of corn are comfortless,
   To tidy that which we egress.
Nine would devote vast wilderness,
For only one species success,
That species needs yet unassess',
Indeed, its numbers are but guess'.
   So, Nine is naught but effervesce,
   Of undue fears and green obsess',
   That mankind should be full' repress',
   While other species coalesce.
Man's liberty, we must confess,
Does not deserve such green caress !
Does not deserve his rights compress',
That other species might progress !
   Mankind should never acquiesce,
   As schemes, which rank unfounded, press !
   The rights of man deserve redress,
   Much more respect, O'blige, No 'blesses !

EEORE

DAME NATURE

Speckled, marbled, striped or dotted,
Brindled, dappled, streaked or spotted,
Fluted, frosted, fringed with roan,
Fluffy, furry, masked full blown,
Muted, grizzled, dark or snowy,
Drab, camouflage or plumage showy,
All critters falling to that lot,
No not deserve a larger plot,
But should be treated equally,
And only by Nature's decree.
For laws by man shall be in vain,
When treating what that DAME ordain !

EEORE

Mr. President
The Green House
Washington, D.C.

Howdy do, Mister President,
Today, from Bare Krick, this note's sent,
As 'spession of our sentiment',
'Bout policies you implement,
And how tax funding, now is spent.
We now know what your "balance" meant !
'Meant only greens get appointment',
To posts of resource management,
Where installed, they betray intent,
'Seek non-disclosure to extent,
Of cloaking all the document',
Of practiced, domain eminent,
On properties in acquisent',
For Uncle Sam's mismanagement,
While greens and those of green descent,
Are subsidized to opulent.
We now know what "new order" meant !
"meant pseudo science rudiment',
That frequently are fraudulent,
And often are undocument',
And totally improvident,
Are now construed intelligent,
For species saving precedent.
       'Meant many 'strictions prevalent,
       With time more issued, unrelent',
       To Liberties full detriment,
       At each and every settlement,
       All across the continent.
'Meant for business, ill portent,
Requiring dollars be misspent,
In vain upon environment,
As species saving supplement,
Which nature renders impotent.

All specie savings are event',
Just gained by natures full consent,
For she alone can pass judgement,
On species saved, or banishment.
Her final word quite permanent!
'Meant homeless and those indigent,
Remain in need for want of rent,
Remain in need of nourishment,
While dollars taxes are oft' misspent,
To promote your green government,
Which claims mankind is negligent,
And makes few bones 'bout their intent,
Of seeking mankinds banishment.
'Economic development,
Restricted, it is evident,
By rules and laws incompetent,
Dictated by green regiment,
With higher sent unemployment,
And unemployed's full discontent,
With causes so envirulent.
When Ag's restricted and prevent',
'Providing of our nutriment,
Many a hungry gal and gent,
Will perceive greens improvident !
Retaining right of free comment,
And right of bearing armament,
Wise use remains yet confident,
That when green schemes 'come evident,
To each and every resident,
Vox populi will sure be vent',
And they will retake government,
Expelling greens expedient,
To stop liberties ravishment.
Drab green, you've came to represent,
Your policies are tesrament,
With economy, you're negligent,
'Private property, 'exigent,
And liberty, you circumvent !

For mankind, you're endangerment !
Wish you hasty retirement,
Preferably 'fore your term ent.
Remaining in full discontent,
On Oregon's coast, where timber went,
In "balance" to your perverse bent !

BELLY ACRES
Bandon by the Sea, OR

SNUFF SNUFF !!

Snuff, the eco dragon lived Wash.,D.C.,
And dabbled in the shady game of taking property.
Little Al and Willie fed that bluster Snuff,
On liberties and properties and taxes they would slough
Together, they would survey critters, bugs and stsuff,
Alas, they're sure to tumble when folkwoe has had enough !

SCIENTIFIC??

Transmitter pulsing in his ear,
Caused Spottie Owl a mortal fear,
And so he flew quite far from where,
The fearful pulse had first appear'.
      Based on this "scientific" test,
      "Ecologists" would launch a quest,
      To set aside much of the west,
      Where only Spotted Owls could nest !
Unmindful of the testing flaws,
Ignoring much of nature's laws,
Seeking only to promote a cause,
And silence logger's power saws !

DEAR 60 MINUTES,

We've got a dragon by the sea,
In hot pursuit of liberty,
I'm tryin' to deal him a blow,
But I'm a novice, you should know,
Mere graduate of Pentaquad,
By way of tooth and nail cum laude,
And must rely on legacy,
Bequeathed by troll, insanity.
    So, should my effort be in vain,
    I'd hope you guys, on call remain,
    For should this dragon every sky,
    We'd need a reg'lar Sigried guy.
And thouth it's Andy, I like best,
That Garfield/Pooh admixture pest,
It's Moe or Curly, I desire,
Or Larry, to fight dragon fire
    For those guys, it's just child's play,
    To face another dragon slay,
    And even out here, in the west,
    We must admit, they are the best !
So, should this dragon ably shield,
All thrusts from pointy pen, I wield,
And keeps on usurping our groun',
Just hop a plane, and come on down !

'Spectively Troo

This letter came back marked "RETURN TO SENDER", which is no surprise when one considers 60 MINUTES slanted programming on ecological issues. I guess the dragon got there first !

Vexing Verse of Vedder

PERMITS

One day Dame Lulu did espy,
A birdies nest in tree on high,
And filled with curiosity,
The Dame began to climb the tree.
Alas, when she had neared the top,
The limb on which she stood went pop.
The Dame then fell below to bush,
With many splinters in her tush.
Was then rushed to emergency,
And placed in care of an M.D.
But with her splinters, long she'd wait,
Before she'd ask the Doc her fate.
Prompted by pain, she then ask why,
Splinter removal was deny'.
Her Doctor then made this reply,
While uttering a woeful sigh,
"First we must secure the permits,
To remove all those old growth bits,
And it's for those that I await,
From B.L.M. and from the State,
From Fish and Wildlife the more,
And many other eco' corps.
Your splinters have 'complication,
Area 'your recreation!"

Vexing Verse of Vedder

THE VADE MECUM OF TREE SHAKING

One day, wee Willie read a book,
Of phobias that Al had brook,
'Bout some ozone depleted nook,
As cause for earth, to someday cook.

Poetic licence, Al partook,
With subject data overlook',
Yet Willie swallowed line and hook,
Quite all of which Al had mistook.

Armed with green cause, Will undertook,
'Strictions via gobledy gook,
That private property be took,
And liberties, of all, forsook.

When TREE OF LIBERTY* is shook,
The rights of people sure are rook' !
Should people gain insightful look,
They seek an end for all such crook' !!

*"TREE OF LIBERTY (Libertarius Taxifolia) is, by far and away, the oldest of old growthes and it alone bears the fruits of liberty. This tree has been enshrined, defended and held in a revered state of pristine preservation through the ages by people who have tested succor from its fruits.

Throughout this trees long history, many have endeavored to deny others its fruit by shaking the tree. When this occurred, those denied invariably assessed the ultimate in taxation upon the greedy perpetrators." Encyclopedia Oregana

Vexing Verse of Vedder

TO THE PRESERVATIONISTS!

To the preservationists who doth,
Prescribe to save the Gypsy Moth,
And set aside the San Joaquin,
To save endangered Med-Fly queen,
And would have the deserts ever bake,
As sole domain for Rattlesnake,
And push for greater wetland swamp,
So more mosquitos, there can romp,
We surely fail to understand,
The "values" of which you demand !

For the world you claim would be pristine,
Has much that we perceive obscene,
Preserving all contagious bugs,
Ticks and spiders, speckled slugs,
Amanitas and poison ivy,
Set asides for toves, all slivey.
For them a wabe as set aside,
Where gyre and gimbel is not denied.
Of you, we fearfully insist,
Are naught but blatant extremist !!

Vexing Verse of Vedder

KAIN'T

Kain't cut your tree, kain't plow your lot,
Until an E.I.S. is wrought.
Kain't mine your creek, kain't graze your cow,
Green regulations won't allow.
Kain't fish no more with nets or reels,
Fish go as prey for increased seals.
Kain't utilize your land for work,
Some unseen species, there may lurk.
Upon your land, you'd best not tread,
Without permission from the Fed',
For some rare bug, you're sure to squash,
It's eco-system rent awash.
At tax time, you must foot the bill,
On land preserved for microbe swill,
'Cause Willie, Al, George, Barb and Bruce,
Have crafted property abuse.
They now crave for non-disclosure,
In shameful effort to obscure,
The methods used to land attain,
With Dragon Eminent Domain !
Seems soon our land will be oppress',
For species by the N.B.S.,
With universal taking, 'less,
Folks realize it's all B.S.
'Cause preservations far and wide,
For all species, 'cept man denied,
Is cause for man, his tax to shrug,
It should be paid by all those bug' !!!

Vexing Verse of Vedder

SMALL WONDER

Called Earth, this pumpkin sphere of ours,
Which orbits in amongst the stars,
In tepid seas, long years ago,
Spawned forms of life that change and grow.

With the ultimate goal that each form reproduce,
While gaining sustenance through the others abuse,
For many are plants that the herbivores munch,
Which in turn the carnivores dine on for lunch.

With the leftover parts, decayed where they've lain,
Providing nutrients, that the plants may sustain.
All forms handicapped with this shameful need,
Of devouring each other or each others seed.

Through the eons of environmental change,
All forms have adapted their habitat range,
Small wonder that timber employees cry foul,
When their resource is threatened to preserve an owl.

For would not habitat adaption occur,
Should owl species no longer have old growth Doug Fir?
Surely adaption occurred in that owls history !
Did that owl not evolve from a form in the sea??

Vexing Verse of Vedder

26

SHAVE AND A HAIRCUT

Wunce upon a time, wee Will,
Spent so much for haircut frill,
That nat-debt when served the bill,
Went asoaring up the hill.
      Then, to hide the haircut trill,
      A green cap was donned by Will.
Woe the green cap did instill,
Naught but portent, very ill,
With rights common rendered nil,
And land taken to fulfill,
Green caps visioned overkill,
For species preservation thrill.
      Man excluded ! Bitter pill !
Mining has been shaved from drill,
Fishers have been shaved from gill,
Timber has been shaved from mill,
Ag's restricted, shaved until,
Little's grown for folks to grill.
Worst of all, green cap would spill,
Folk liberties, shaved to nil.
That appears too high a bill,
For human species to fulfill,
Preserving every rock and rill,
For naught but green cap specie swill !!

Vexing Verse of Vedder

The following rhyme was plagiarized from pop's personal letter dated 8-9-1922. It well exemplifies the fact that agriculturists have long exhibited concerns for the environment, and practiced as good stewards regarding eco-systems.

We've bathed the bossie's tootsies, we've cleaned the roosters ears,
We've trimmed the turkey's wattles with antiseptic shears.

With talcum, all the guinea hens are beautiful and bright,
And Dobbin's wreath of gleaming teeth, we've burnished snowy white.

With pungent sachet powder, we've glorified the dog,
And when we have the leisure, we'll manicure the hog.

We've done all in our power, to have a barn de luxe,
We've dipped the sheep in eau de rose, we've sterilized the ducks,

The little chicks are daily fed on sanitated worms,
The calves and colts are always boiled, to keep them free from germs,

And thoroughly to carry out our prophylactic plan,
Next week, we think, we shall begin to wash the hired man.

Vexing Verse of Vedder's Pop

NEEDED!

Preservationists requisition,
Private property acquisition,
With pseudo sciences position,
That saving species as tradition,
Is grand and noble by design.

Yet any in depth inquisition,
Of pseudo sciences position,
And private land acquisition,
Shows liberty in full perdition,
And common rights of all malign'.

Preservationists acquisition,
Of funding through the land transition,
Provides them with more ammunition,
To forward errant thought position,
And grasp more land of yours and mine.

What's needed now is legislition,
To terminate the acquisition,
And restrict errant thought position,
Which fosters liberties perdition,
That liberty might once more shine !!

Vexing Verse of Vedder

OWL CONDITIONING

(Or The Science Of Finger Pointing)

From lofty limb, at beck and call,
The Spotted Owls are summoned, all,
To feast upon some mousy pall,
In name of "research", broad and tall,
Throughout the northwest timber sprawl !

Conditioned thus for food depend',
By owls upon their "research" friend (?),
Will surely, for the owls, but tend,
A lessened need for them to fend,
About their realm for food content',
And ultimately does portend,
The owls extinction in the end !

Then, those that go by research name,
To maintain their research acclaim,
Will produce some research that frame,
Statistics which will point the blame,
For owls demise, and all the shame,
On all folks in the logging game !!

Vexing Verse of Vedder

GREEN GROW THE DRAGONS

While the king, every morning, trots all 'round the hill,
His legate counts species at each rock and rill,
Sadly this survey is all buy-ill-logic-kill,
And financed with tax funds, the twain seek to spill,

> Tra, la, la; Tra, la, lee, lee; My taxes fulfill,
> The schemes of the greenies on Capital Hill !

Green grow the dragons on Capitol Hill,
Their purses grow greener with greater tax bill,
With "non-profit helpers" subsidized still,
In land acquisitions, the dragons fulfill.

> Tra, la, la; Tra, la, lee, lee; It gives me a chill,
> To wake up in the morning, with properties nil !

Sadly, for humans, their plan does instill,
A full loss of liberties, rendered to nil,
While the dragons execute E.S.A. will,
And implement the N.B.S. codicil.

> Tra, la, la; Tra, la, lee, lee; It's the dragons will,
> That Earth be devoted for non-human swill !

Vexing Verse of Vedder

METHINKS!

Methinks that our posterity,
Shall lack the opportunity,
Of any chance that they might see,
A Spotted Owl that's wild and free !

Owls now respond to call command,
to be "rewarded", fed by hand,
By seekers who don't understand,
Effects conditioned by demand !

Those seeking data to collect,
On Spotted Owls, they would protect,
Have demonstrated their neglect,
Of effected cause and caused effect !

With preservation they're so rapt',
Conditioning owls to thus adapt,
Hand fed behavior is sure apt,
To cause the species to be zapped !

And so this plan they pioneer,
In quest of more owls to revere,
Will cause the owls to disappear,
'Cause Nature's plan they interfere !!

Vexing Verse of Vedder

JUST IN CASE!

Discoveries in Oregon have been made quite recently,
Of happenings, from long ago, in man's pre-history,
It seems a feathered critter had stopped to take a rest,
And there she found a likely mound to clear and build a nest,
With beak and talon, from the mound, a hollow she did scratch,
Then laid one large and lonesome egg, which she would later hatch,
The chick, when hatched, possessed of such voracious appetite,
It kept the mother scavenging all day and half the night,
Legend tells us that the feeding had the circumstance,
The menu preferred by the chick, was that of elephants,
Perhaps by now you realize, the size you should take stock,
For the next site was Mazama, and the critter was a Roc,
With colored plumage splendor, 'twas the flying paragon,
That put to shame the birdies lame, so prized by Audobon.
The nest site now is flooded, Crater Lake the nomenclature,
And Tablerock a gizzard stone, the chick spit back to nature.
Now that set aside priorities are our number one concern,
Should we not set aside America, in case the Roc return?

Vexing Verse of Vedder

33

WHAT DO I SMELL?

Fe, Fi, Fo, Fum, Willies kingdom,
Sets policy in a vacuum,
And Willies Interior chum,
With non—disclosure, would stay mum,
Of proprietors that succumb,
Their properties to species, glum,
While greens are tossed a pretty plum.

Meanwhile, liberty is benumb,
Her folkish fruit kept under thumb,
With specie surveys cumbersome,
By tax support from deaf and dumb.

But, when these rivers have been swum,
And all folks tire of the thrum,
Well surely then a time will come,
When some will rise to beat the drum !!

                                        Vexing Verse of Vedder

GIST!

How many Spotted Owls exist?
Do they number quite a grist?
How have they managed to subsist?
What habitat do they resist?
How many owls were there in hist'?
How many do we need assist?
If some should go, will they be missed?
What number should owl count consist?
Should timber suffer eco' tryst?
Are answers shrouded in a mist?

It's now the time we should desist,
Promoted plans of "naturalist" !

It's also time we should insist,
That own and man now co-exist !

Should claims for set asides persist,
From thoughtless eco' activist',
By way of "science" they would twist,
Man then will head endangered list !

Vexing Verse of Vedder

NUMBERFUL BUY-ILL-LOGIC-KILL SURVEY

Ol' Bruce Bonkers managed land, I C D EEK O,
And on that land, he counted worms, I C D EEK O,
With a worm hole here, and a worm hole there,
Hither holes, thither holes, Brucie's count is full of holes !
I C DRAGON WOE !
Ol' Bruce Bonkers managed land, I C D EEK O,
And on that land, he counted beasts, I C D EEK O,
With a beastie here, and a beastie there,
Oft' a beast, made a feast, of some beast, yet undeceased !
I C DRAGON WOE !
Ol;' Bruce Bonkers managed land, I C D EEK O,
And on that land, he counted plants, I C D EEK O,
With an implant here, and replant there,
Yon a plant, gone a plant, everywhere a misplant !
I C DRAGON WOE !
Ol; Bruce Bonkers managed land, I C D EEK O,
And on that land he counted birds, I C D EEK O,
With a bird flew here, and a bird flew there,
Her birds flew, there birds flew, everywhere bird do-do flew !
I C DRAGON WOE !
Ol' Bruce Bonkers managed land, I C D EEK O,
And on that land, he counted bugs, I C D EEK O,
With a big bite here, and a bug bite there,
Here bugs munch, there bugs crunch, Brucie's count is 'out to lunch',
I C DRAGON WOE ! C I TOLD U SO !

Vexing Verse of Vedder

36

DRAGON, SPECIES RUES
THE GREEN HOUSE
WASHINGTON, D.C.

Not so very dear Dragon Rues,
Your thoughts, I've throughly peruooze',
And recognize that you're inthuooze',
With plans to take Miss Public cruooze',
Whereby, Miss Public, you might wooze,
With flowered words, which may induooze,
Miss Public to become so looze,
That you might sweep her from her shuooze,
And ultimately, might seduooze.
      But yet, Miss Public still might chuooze,
      To not avail herself so luooze,
      Should she occaision to peruooze,
      Her friend, Miss Liberty's abuooze.
While we await Miss Public's vuooze,
We'd surely hope that you would chuooze,
To rectify all ills you duooze,
And cease Miss Liberty's abuooze.
      Now, as to all those ills you duooze,
      They include property's abuooze,
      And regulations of its uooze,
      Or taking it with specie ruooze.
They include human rights abuooze,
Denying folks their rights to chuooze,
By way of pseudo science "nuooze",
That you politically misuooze.
      I yet remain, untrooly yuooze,
      At Bandon, Oregon, County Coos.

Vexing Verse of Vedder

AGE OF HYPOCRISY?

In pre-history, we long have known,
One early era as age of stone,
And when that era was rendered non's,
There followed closely, the age of bronze.
Not long after Nero had fiddle',
Came ages we all know as middle.
We've Age of Fable; and Chivalry,
Both are authored by Bullfinch decree.
Wharton gave us Age of Innocence,
A tale styled in eloquence.
And Age of Reason, by people gain',
From studied effort of Thomas Paine.

One wonders just how our present age,
Will be perceived by some future sage,
When our "history" has circumspect,
Of advantaged view in retrospect.
For it surely seems that future man,
Will better grasp and full understan',
That at present time, when man knew not,
How many species the Earth had got,
And knew little how they interact,
Yet prone to accept much fable as fact,
And knew quite little of each specie,
Including each species quantity,
That man would be so presumptuous,
Of saving all those unknown, from us.

Vexing Verse of Vedder

From a sign on the gate at Belly Acres:

HALT!

Advancing further, please desist,
Until the following you wist.
NO peddling peddlers who persist,
Their wares are such, we can't resist !
NO bible thumping moralists,
Or tax assessing optimists !
NO politician vocalists,
Or gloomy, doomy pessimists !
NO Liberty antagonists,
Environmental activists,
Private property acquisists,
Or specie preservationists !
NO ill begotten alchemists,
Or pot plantation colonists !
NO acts of pseudo scientists,
Or save the planet extremists !
NO boonjie seeking lover trysts,
Or unclad, streaking egotists !
It is our hope, we can subsist,
And well, without above, exist !
So, should you not be on our list,
You're welcome here, we do insist !!

Vexing Verse of Vedder

JOUST THE WINDMILL

It is not right, so it would seem,
To lay Nat debt, by crook or scheme,
On progeny far down the stream,
Now but in grandson's eyes, a gleam.

It's always been the Fed's design,
To whip the masses into line,
By inflating the dollar sign,
And take away what's yours and mine.

Fed's history for duration,
Oft' increasing the inflation,
Robs common folk's predestination.
Gross injustice situation !

Fed yet suffers no restriction,
Limiting or interdiction,
Their dollar arithmetiction,
Which they suffer much addiction.

Fixed income folk are first to dread,
The power weilded by Fed,
That sucks them dry 'fore they are dead,
And leaves estates far in the red.

Seems shameful that retired folk,
Who long have toiled in the yoke,
Should savings lose and then go broke,
'Cause Fed would engineer such stroke

So folk should seek to rectify,
All which Fed windmill would deny,
And joust the mill for funds he'd shy,
That better life you yet might buy

Vexing Verse of Vedder

NOWHERE!

The decade of the nineties has arrived and with it brought,
Quantities of perplexities spawned by errant thought,
That vast set asides not be denies for tiny owls with spot' !
Yet, if looking to the brighter side, our blessings we take stock
That preservationists are not learning to turn back the clock,
Or we'd likely be providing realm for some durn pristine Roc !
Then the human foe would sure attempt of all the earth to con,
As set aside to save Roc's hide as demand' by Audobon',
With nowhere left on earth for folks to build and live upon !

OREFOLK WOE

Not long ago, Orefolk did strive,
To reduce tax with measure five,
Its failure wrought by those connive',
To keep big govament alive.
    No tax reduction has ensued,
    Yet greater tax bills have accrued,
    Which leads the Orefolk to conclude,
    That once again, they've been delude'
Tax escalation has but slowed,
Pro-escalators seek to goad,
Orefolk to increase their tax load,
With Measure One, a new tax mode.
    With one more mode to grow and grow,
    Orefolk will have more tax they owe,
    Big govamint will get the dough,
    To foster greater Orefolk woe !

THE TEST

The will possessed by liberty,
Does not defend her destiny !
That chore is left summarily,
For each and every one of we !
    Sure' none would damage liberty,
    Lest it was done unwittingly !
    So when such damage does commence,
    It's left to others, her defence !
Can those remaining 'stride the fence,
Be rallied yet, in her defence?
Can change be wraught in unwits sense,
By small degree of eloquence

RECIPE FOR LIBERTY—

Ingredients:

Rights—

1. Life
2. Liberty
3. Property
4. Citizenship
5. Vote
6. Assembly
7. Petition
8. Just compensation
9. Keep, bear arms
10. Due process
11. Equal protection
12. To pay taxes

Freedoms—

1. Speech
2. Religion
3. Press

Freedoms from—

1. Involuntary servitude
2. Excessive bail & fines
3. Unusual punishment
4. Double jeopardy
5. Unreasonable search & seizure

Toss one schepel each of rights 1 through 11 into a huge container and stir until well mixed. One at a time, add and fold in, one anker each of freedoms. In a separate container, blend together one anker each of freedoms from, slowly spoon this blend into your rights and freedoms mixture but do not stir. Place an airtight cover over your mix. Carry right # 12 downwind a minimum distance of ten miles and cast an infinitesimal amount to the wind. Return to your mix and after taking precautionary steps to assure that the wind has not shifted, remove the airtight cover and leaven your mixture with one sunbeam. This leavening is not only all enlightening, it also provides your mix with the feature that whenever you partake of your liberty, more will rise to replace it. Indeed, you can have your liberty and partake it too ! ENJOY !

Vexing Verse of Vedder

TO THE "OTHER GUYS"!

The Eco'-manics 'cross this land,
Universal in their demand,
As each, in turn, posess' the nerve,
That "others" pay for their preserve!
    Example? Sure, we've not seen yet,
    North Indiana back to wet',
    Nor any move by Jontz for same,
    Seem's "others" forests are his game !
For their preserves, by hue and cry,
The rights of "others", they'd deny,
Full disregarding costs so high,
'Cause they're borne by the "other guy"!
    Seem's time is nigh, that "other guys",
    Take full heed and seek to devise,
    Fitting reward that they deserve,
    A Preservationist preserve !
With access demanded direct,
For Eco'-manic intellect !
Sure, "other guys" would then be free,
From their perverse indignity !!

Vexing Verse of Vedder

Tomarrow

Dear Uncle Sam,

We, the undersigned, hold these truths to be self evident :

1. That unparalleled demands have manifested which greatly heighten the need that the United States of America and all possessions be declared an Eminent Domain Free Zone.

2. That political agendas of "non-profit" organizations no longer be funded by subsidies from governmental agencies in the land acquisition process.

3. That "non-profit" organizations be duly taxes for all profits accrued form trafficing in any commodity or real estate.

4. That measures of environmental or ecological restriction or regulation may be implemented only after the following parameters have been met :

    I.   Appropriate filing of ECONOMICAL IMPACT STATEMENTS

    II. APPROPRIATE FILING OF HUMAN LIBERTY IMPACT STATEMENTS

    III. *VALID* scientific documentation of the measures need

    IV. An approving ballot taken from all citizens

5. That Federal taxes lower each year by a percentage equal to the ratio of the golden mean multiplied by ten to the power of minus one (6.18035 %)

NAME (print)   ADDRESS   SIGNATURE

_____

_____

_____

_____

_____

Vexing Verse of Vedder

Dear Audie Bonn,

How many trees should a murrelet get if that murrelet is scarlet yet?

How high a parapet should that scarlet murrelet get as a minaret so his soul abet'?

If that scarlet murrelet met a murrelet coquette with violet aigrette and they began curvet, would that be cause to fret 'bout what they might beget?

If that murrelet coquette with the violet aigrette brought along her soubrette as black as jet, would it be good etiquette for the jet soubrette to tempt or whet the scarlet murrelet from the murrelet coquette to engage in curvet?

If the murrelet coquette with the violet aigrette got in a sweat about the jet soubrette and the scarlet murreleet engaging in curvet, would the scarlet murrelet throw the jet soubrette out in the wet so the coquette not fret?

When finished with curvet, does the scarlet murrelet ever smoke a cigarette?

Would it be a good bet that your wry-sci-set net nary an answer yet?

Vexing Verse of Vedder

WHERE?

Someone, whose faculties have quit,
Has deemed that we should now submit,
All old growth forests, exquisite,
That owls with spots might benefit,
And of our land, we should commit,
For owls a space near infinite,
Manhattan Island would permit,
A space for only six to flit,
And all the land on Earth admit,
But sixteen million owls to fit.
Somehow, that seems like quite a bit,
Of land per owl, to be remit !
And should the owl gain perquisite,
To all the land on Earth, to wit,
Where will the people be transmit'??????

Vexing Verse of Vedder

PRO AND CON

During the nineties, it was Pro,
With pseudo science coined to show,
That "threatened" species wouldn't grow,
Without preserves, row after row.

Remains a relict, name of CON,
Who, through the ages, rose at dawn,
To study all that knowledge spawn,
From which, conclusions he had drawn.

By preserves that PRO depicted,
CON felt fully interdicted,
And CON's liberties restricted,
By PRO's interests, so conflicted.

PRO would then lobby at the State,
His master plan to legislate,
A circumstance that would create,
A need for PRO and CON debate.

PRO "We surely must preserve the Earth,
        In all it's breadth, and all it's girth,
        That progeny of future birth,
        Enjoy the bounty and the worth."

CON "If all the Earth, full far and wide,
        Is naught but species set-aside,
        With liberty for man denied,
        Where will man's progeny abide?"

PRO "The species that we seek to save,
        With set-asides, of which we crave,
        Are those whose outlook is but grave.
        We must control how men behave!"

CON "Of species you seek to 'restore',
        You know not quant' that went before,
        Or what is 'needed' evermore.
        Your specie data, I deplore!"

PRO "That's why we need N. B. Survey,
        To gain the data, we can weigh,
        Of which species are in decay,
        To be protect' in NATURE'S WAY!"

CON "It always has been nature's way,
        To test each specie, day by day,
        With 'dapting species 'lowed to stay,
        And others, by extinction, slay!"

PRO "But we must save them from that fate,
        And nurse them to a healthy state,
        On the preserves that we create,
        Where nature's way is imitate'!"

CON "Tis obvious you don't perceive,
        That nature does not grant reprieve !
        Those 'dapting, extensions receive,
        And those that fail, all get the heave!"

PRO "But we should save them if we can,
        Assuring species not be ban',
        On properties we take from man !
        That is our visioned master plan!"

CON "Your master plan does not hold 'wet',
        By nature's law all life is threat',
        To life adapting, life is let ;
        That unadapting, doom beset!"

PRO "That's why we have the E.S.A.,
        A law that species doomed, gain sway,
        O'er what you claim is NATURE'S WAY,
        That species might have brighter day!"

CON "My claim, Earth's records do maintain,
     Of specie loss and specie gain,
     And laws of men are all in vain,
     When treating what NATURE ORDAIN !
     'Twas you who, early on, sought sway,
     By using term of 'NATURE'S WAY',
     Seem's your own terms have gone astray,
     Your visioned master plan betray'!"
Long after, PRO would fonch and fit,
His master plan, he would not quit.
Adamantly, he'd not admit,
'Twas much CON said, he didn't git.
     Con took his debate win in stride,
     He knew when laws of men collide,
     With those that nature had applied,
     That only nature would decide.

                              Vexing Verse of Vedder

MY TURN!

Some folks, these days, are sure inclined
To speak in terms, all undefined,
For it seems often, that we find,
Such term that's artfully designed,
To exploit favor from mankind.
Thus, "ECOSYSTEM" comes to mind,
With definition unassigned,
And much suggestive all entwined.

Of that term, Webster did not know,
And Funk and Wagnalls does not show,
Nor Encyclopedias stow,
Or any histories bestow,
A line of writ for long ago,
Or even yesterday, I trow.
No "ECOSYSTEM" high or low,
Betwixt, between or back and fro !

This term was coined, 'cause it suggest',
That preserve creed be manifest,
And private property be wrest,
As set aside for specie next,
While liberties are put to test,
By regulations, ranked abreast,
From definition unexpressed,
By those in "ECOSYSTEM" quest !

Since coining terms, bring some such glee,
Perhaps we should have coining spree,
And all share in that cup of tea,
Without a care what they decree,
Devoid of meaning referee,
With definitions, absentee.
So, when a turn comes 'round to me,
My choice : BIOPERVERSITY !!

Vexing Verse of Vedder

54

ONLY ONE!

'Tis said too many cooks have fault,
For pooridge that is naught but salt,
And birdies few are thought the best,
As many birdies foul the nest.
And for yard work we should employ,
The services of just one boy,
'Cause if another one we pay,
The two of them will only play.

Pray tell, why are so many sent,
To play at running government?
Would not there be less room to err,
If only one was sent up there?
Should only one not be hard pressed,
To spend as much as all the rest??

Vexing Verse of Vedder

HOO, HOO, HOO?

Hoo says that forests for multiple use,
Should be restricted for an owls abuse?
Hoo said that owls need an empire to flit,
So big, that Manhattan but six owls would fit?
Or twice the number, that's now estimate',
Would totally fill the Hoosier State?
Or but sixteen million owls could berth,
On all the landed mass on Earth? Hoo, Hoo?

Vexing Verse of Vedder

HANSEL & GRENDEL (A FAIRY TALE?)

The characters :

Hansel—   Lost Liberties, that he'd adore',
              From legacy of those before,
              Lost properties, he'd title bore,
              To earn his sustenance, the more.
              This farmer set out to restore,
              His liberties from days of yore,
              By wading through the dragon gore . . . .

Grendel—   Folk Liberties, this Grendel bled,
              Folk properties, caused to be fled,
              Destroyed folk right to earn their bread,
              With regulations in their stead,
              He'd implement by many head'.
              Everyone, who's Beowulf read,
              Knows Grendel is a beast to dread!

The plot: Much Grendel sought to non-disclose,
              For fear the knowledge would expose,
              The means and power, which he rose,
              To cause folk liberties be froze',
              And properties to be foreclose',
              With regulations he'd impose',
              To save some species, he had chose !

The story: Wunce upon a time . . . . . .
              (Sorry folks, this story remains in progress.)

                                Vexing Verse of Vedder

Yesterday

Dear Uncle Sam,

Just thought I'd drop a line to say,
We're lookin' for a brighter day,
'Cause much of what, today we see,
Bodes ill for all our liberty'.

The guy you've hired recently,
The rest of us, to oversee,
Leaves a good deal to be desired,
And 'twould be best if he were fired.

"Balance", "New Order", were his claim',
Yet all unbalance is his game,
For ALL his 'pointments, we can see,
Are from but one faction only.

His choice for King Interior,
A chap naught but inferior,
Now has all of his agencies,
Worshiping unknown deities.

And now would undertake the chore,
That Mother Nature's always bore,
By spending tax funds that we pay,
On Buy-ill-logic-kill Survey.

He further has his agencies,
Usurping private properties,
And pays his pals vast subsidies,
For "help", in these atrocities.

'Cause Audubon Society,
And the Nature Conservancy,
And other groups of the same ilk,
Have crafted plans, tax funds to milk.

For they line up, all dewy eyed,
Behind you, on purse pocket side,
Their grasping hand, when e'er you blink,
Deep in that pocket, has been slink'.

But, that's not all that we decry,
Which stems from your new' hired guy,
He 'pears inept to navigate,
A course that's true, for ship of state.

For launching of our state was based,
On liberty remaining chaste,
With rights of private property,
Integral part of liberty.

Yet, this guy'd property restrict,
And liberty, he'd interdict,
For reason of some visioned cause,
By premise of weird science flaws.

And Congress? Sure' you know by now,
Each member has their sacred cow,
Which precludes they accomplish much,
Hence, liberty is left besmutch'.

Then, too, we've congressmen with flaws,
Of 'cepting funds from errant cause,
Who then, that errant cause promote,
By manner of their purchased vote.

Thus, funds that you have taxed from we,
From your pocket 'come absentee,
To purchase laws which disagree,
That we should maintain liberty.

So, we'd like to voice our druthers,
That state's ship be steered by others,
With common sense enough to know,
To steer full wide these reefs of woe.

Please guard the state ship, aft and prow,
And I will run along for now.
Perhaps sometime, I'll write ag'in,
Should 'spression rights not be deemed sin.

Vexing Verse of Vedder

About the author:

HEREDITARY?

My ancestor, tenth generation,
Suffered the humiliation,
Made public in a reprimand,
From Colve, then governor of the land,
For failed respect to Albany,
While sheriff of Schenectady,
Sixteen hundred seventy three.

Could be the traits inherited,
When disrespect is merited,
'Cause I've developed through the years,
A pressing urge to burn the ears,
Of those whose actions do affect,
The rights of others, they'd neglect,
Where liberty is circumspect !

Vexing Verse of Vedder

HOW MUCH?

If Spotted Owls deserve a realm,
In size, the mind to overwhelm,
What acreage, in your opinion,
Should go for Dappled Dutch dominion?
'Cause now the acreage precedent,
For Spotted Owls, that has been spent,
Should indicate vast set aside,
For Dappled Dutch, not be denied !
How vast a set aside is need',
By Brindled Briton or Striped Swede,
By Dotted Dane or Speckled Scot
By Marbled Roan of Hotentot,
A German Grizzled, a Frenchman Fringed,
A Snowy Serb or a Spaniard Singed?
How large a set aside will be,
Full realized by humanity?

Vexing Verse of Vedder

EXCEPT!

It sure seems that preservationists,
Of earth would make a zoo,
With ample room for critters all,
Except for me and you !

Vexing Verse of Vedder

MUCH MORE IN COMMON!

Many times, we have noticed the fact that both
politicians and felons are serving time. IN
due time we recognize that often times the two
have much more in common !

Vexing Verse of Vedder

1994
FOLKWOE
CALENDAR
NOW YOU SEE US
NOW YOU DON'T!
WAIT'll WE GET
NON-disclosure!

WEBSTIR'S FOLKWOE LEXICON

ECOCISTERN : (1) A fetid cesspool that foments conclusion drawn from unfounded premise. (2) An area which spawns and nurtures those prerequisites that cause groundless hypotheses to become fecund and proliferate.

ECOCYSTEM : that which materializes as a sac of morbid matter, which strives to infect the rights and liberties of all humankind. A term that, from want of definition, is often misspelled.

ECODRAGON : An entity with many heads that by promoting ecocystems from the ecocisterns, deserves the full contempt of folk yet fond of property & liberty.

ECOLOGY : A science that has conveniently been omitted by the ecocisterns.

ECONOMY : That which is precluded by ecocystem.

ECOSPECIES : A fertile bio-bunch.

ECOTONE : That which can be sensed both by sound and by smell as one nears an ecocystem.

ECOTYPE : Those types that espouse the cause of ecocisterns by promoting ecocystems. SYN : Ecodragon.

ECRASEUR : An instrument used to remove ecocystem tumors. It severs the heads of ecodragons by the gradual tightening of a wire loop.

ECSTASY : A worldly state which is devoid of ecocisterns, ecocystems, ecodragons, and ecotypes, with ecraseurs obsolete.

A LETTER EDGED IN GREEN:

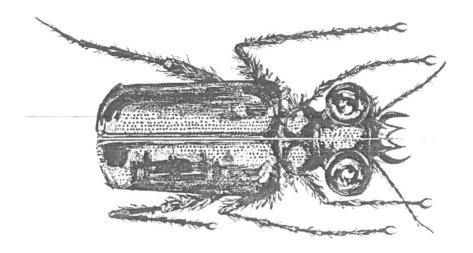

Any Day Now

John Q. Public
Main Street
United States
America zapcode

Dear John,

As the Brindled Bloodsucker has recently been placed high on the endangered species list, we have decided to dedicate your land as habitat ecosystem for the Bloodsucker's preservation.

You are herby advised to forfeit your title and vacate your property, but before you go, there is the matter of your retroactive property tax, which we need, that appropriate compensation for our non-profit acquisition helpers might be implemented. Follow these directions carefully :

1. In one and the same envelope, place both your retroactive tax payment and your property title.

2. Address the envelope to: Campfire
Department of Interior Abruce
Washington, DC

3. Promptly vacate your premises.

4. Drop our letter in the first mailbox as you leave.

Campfire Cronies

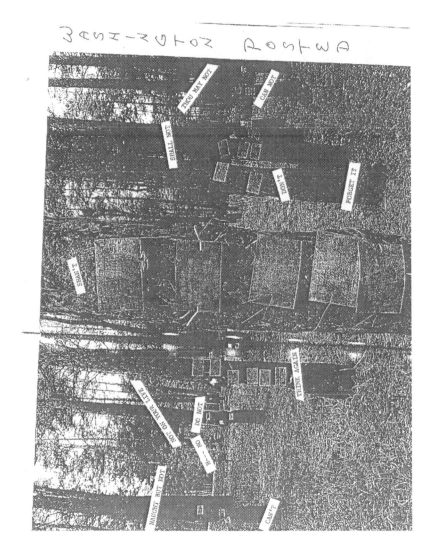

WASHINGTON POSTWA

70

VOLUME II

EE·ORE'S
LIBERTY RAG

A FREE PRESS, IMPLEMENTING FLEXIBLE POLICIES
AND FLEXIBLE PRINTING SCHEDULES ALL FLEXABLY
PUBLISHER . . . . . . I. TROLL
EDITOR . . . . . TWIRK
ASSISTANT EDITOR . . . EE-ORE
GOPHER & FLUNKIE . . LEONARD VEDDER
ADDRESS RT. 2, BOX 570, BANDON, OREGON 97411

Dedicated to LIBERTY'S PRESERVANCY
As opposed to Nature Conservancy
Published by Troll Enterprises
Located under the Bear Creek Bridge

We dusted off EEORE'S newspaper and here we is again bringing
you the latest newsworthy tidbits and some that are older than
dirt.

In this issue is: A supplement to "O YE GODS"

                     Verses on holidays

                     Reprints from 1994 WOEPOLK CALENDAR

                     Common History

                     Uncommon History

                     Copies of old letters

                     Writ having to do with this area

          And tributes on: Spuds

                                 Apples

                                 Cranberries

                                 and others

EEORE disclaims any and all x-rated stuff herein contained.   All
x-rated stuff was due to the insistance of the INSANE TROLL.   A
few years ago, a friend said no to the TROLL and no one has seen
him since.   Consequently it is our policy to never say NO to the
INSANE TROLL .

LIBERTY RAG

===

A FREE PRESS, IMPLEMENTING
FLEXIBLE POLICIES

AND FLEXIBLE PRINTING
SCHEDULES ALL FLEXIBLY

PUBLISHER . . . . . . I. TROLL

EDITOR . . . . . . TWINK

ASSISTANT . . . . EE-ORE
EDITOR

GOPHER & . . . LEONARD
FLUNKIE VEDDER

ADDRESS RT. 2 BOX 570, BANDON,
OREGON 97411

Dedicated to
LIBERTY'S
PRESERVANCY
As opposed to Nature
Conservancy Published
by Troll Enterprises
Located under the Bear
Creek Bridge

We dusted off EEORE'S newspaper and here we is again bringing you the latest newsworthy tidbits and some that are older than dirt.

In this issue is: Verses on holidays
Common History
Uncommon History
Copies of old letters
Writ having to do with this area

And tributes on: Spuds
Apples
Cranberries
and others

EEORE disclaims any and all x-rated stuff herein contained. All x-rated stuff was due to the insistence of the INSANE TROLL. A few years ago, a friend said no to the TROLL and no one has seen him since. Consequently it is our policy to never say NO to the INSANE TROLL.

THE MAKING OF A TRAITOR

Benedict Arnold, born Norwich, Connecticut on January 14, 1741. By 1762 he was a druggist and bookseller at New Haven with some general trade business with Canada and the West Indies. 1767 he wed Margaret Mansfield, subsequently had 3 sons.

5/3/1775 he was a Colonel of militia sent to seize Fort Ticonderoga. With but few recruits he joined Ethan Allen and his Green Mountain Boys. Together they forced the surrender of Fort Ti on 5/10/1775. Arnold then took 100 men, sailed to north end of Lake Champlain and captured Fort St. John.

June '75 Mrs. Arnold died, sons subsequently reared by Hannah, the sister of Arnold. Arnold returned to what was now the Continental Army commanded by G. Washington and proposed an expedition through the Maine wilderness to attack Quebec in conjunction with the invasion of Montreal already planned. In Sept. '75 with 1,100 men and under incredible hardships, Arnold's march north is a classic in military history. Nov. 11 reached St. Lawrence River, but men were too exhausted to attack Quebec. Montgomery took Montreal on Nov. 12 then joined forces with Arnold. Dec. 31 In a blinding snowstorm they conducted an unsuccessful assault on Quebec. Montgomery was killed, Arnold wounded in knee. Despite his wound, Arnold extricated his troops and maintained a tight blockade during the winter. Celebrated as a hero, congress promoted Arnold to brigadier General Jan. 10, 1776. May '76 British reinforcements under Gen. Carleton broke Arnold's siege of Quebec and he was forced to retreat. Carleton pursued Arnold intending to invade N.Y. as far as Albany. Brit. Gen. Howe was to capture N.Y. City and control the Hudson resulting in New England colonies severed from the others. Divide and conquer! With great energy, tenacity and ingenuity, Arnold delayed the northern invasion by stubborn resistance to Lake Champlain which forced Carlton to make time consuming preparations. Arnold had built a fleet of crude ships and at Valcour Island Nov. 11, 1776 fought the superior British fleet to a draw. Arnold's force escaped in the night and were forced to scuttle their crude fleet but they had been successful in discouraging Carleton who went back to Canada. Once again Arnold was a celebrated hero. He was ordered to Rhode Island to oppose the British who had seized Newport. Try as he might, Arnold could not gather enough troops for his assignment. Feb. 1777, congress promoted 5 brigadiers to major generals, all were junior in rank to Arnold. He was justly incensed and even Washington complained of the injustice at the same time persuading Arnold not to resign. Visiting his home, Arnold learned of a British raid on Danbury, he dashed to the scene, rallied some militia and harassed the retreating enemy. Congress promoted him to Major General but *did not* restore his seniority. In fact congress began questioning Arnolds accounts from Canada and in disgust he resigned. Washington persuaded him to withdraw his resignation in order to take command of the militiamen under Maj. Gen Schuyler. Schuyler would command the regulars. Again the British plan was divide and conquer, with Gen. Burgoyne's large army moving to Albany via Lake Champlain, Howe's large army moving up the Hudson and Lt. Col. St. Leger was to disembark at Osego and sweep down the Mohawk Valley to Albany. Schuyler sent Arnold with 1,000 men to relieve Fort Schuyler (formerly Fort Stanwix) near Rome, N.Y. which was under siege by St. Leger's force. Arnold used a ruse, sending news that he was coming with a vast army. St. Leger's Indians deserted and his tories soon followed, St. Leger retreated. Returning to headquarters, Arnold found that Maj. Gen. Horatio Gates had succeeded Schuyler in command. Having virtually no combat experience, Gates had gained his command by way of political intrigues in congress. Having considerable combat experience, Arnold no doubt felt unjustly snubbed. Americans Fortified Bemis Heights near Stillwater, as the best defensive position to check Burgoynes advance. Sept. 19, '77 Battle was joined at Freemans Farm with Arnold commanding the left wing. With his impetuous nature, Arnold his men attack, forcing Gates into a greater general action than he preferred. Both sides claimed victory but the British lost twice as many men. In his report to congress, Gates omitted all mention of Arnold. When Arnold objected, Gates removed him from command of the left wing. Lacking authority, Arnold remained in camp and on Oct. 7, '77 the British again attacked. Americans meet the assault and successfully turned the British flanks but British center stood firm. Arnold then appeared on the scene without any authority beyond the enthusiasm caused by his appearance, rallied the men and broke the

British center. Arnold's horse was killed and he was again wounded in the leg that had been wounded at Quebec. Arnold was carried a hero to a hospital in Albany. Burgoyne began a laborious retreat ending with his surrender on Oct. 17, '77. In May '78 Arnold joined Washington at Valley Forge, and was assigned to command at Philadelphia. On May 30, Arnold took the oath required of officers, acknowledging the Declaration of Independence and renouncing all allegiance to King George III. Arnold's extravagant life style and his friendliness with torys caused patriots to become disgusted and aroused suspicions. His need of money to maintain his desired social standing caused him to secretly enter a partnership to profit from temporary closing of Philadelphia shops, to buy an interest in two ship cargoes of doubtful propriety, and to seek a forfeited loyalist estate in N.Y. At the same time he donated $500 for the support of the children of Maj. Gen. Joseph Warren who had been killed at Bunker Hill. In Apr. '79 Arnold married Peggy Shippen, daughter of a tory and they eventually had 3 sons and 1 daughter. Arnold resigned his military governorship in the face of accusations that he had misused public property and authority. Washington's delay in setting a date for his court martial made Arnold violent and unreasonable. May '79 Arnold sent an emissary to N.Y. offering traitorous services to the British which was accepted. For 5 months, Arnold sent encoded military intelligence to the British. In Dec. '79 Arnold had his long delayed court martial resulting in a verdict that found Arnold guilty of using army wagons to haul private goods and illegally granting a pass to a trading ship. Sentenced to receive a reprimand form Washington. Arnold asked retired Gen. Schuyler and other friends to recommend him for command of West Point. Gaining that command he offered surrender of West Point to the British, and he also betrayed the Americans projected expedition to Canada. Upon learning of the Sept. 21/22, '80 capture of British Maj. Andres with incriminating evidence, Arnold escaped down the Hudson to the British. Following the surrender of Cornwallis Oct. '81 at Yorktown, Arnold, Peggy and children shipped to London. He died 1801, Peggy died 1804. All 6 of Arnold's sons served with distinction in the British army.

All of the foregoing was taken from Encyclopedia Americana.

The following is from "The Book Of Lists" by Wallechinsky, Wallace and Wallace in which they list General Horatio Gates among the ten *worst* Generals in history.

At the battle of Saratoga, the American commanding general Gates fought more with his subordinate Benedict Arnold than with the British. Gates had almost no military experience had received his command due to political intrigue in Congress. During the fighting, Gates refused to leave the safety of his fortified camp and ordered his men to remain inactive. Arnold disobeyed him and engaged the British. During the critical battle of Bemis Heights, Gates sat in his tent and argued the merits of the American revolutionary cause with a captured British officer, While Arnold defeated the British army. Gates later lost the battle of Camden (1780) and was dismissed from the army.

The historical novel "Saratoga" published in 2005 was written by David Garland a British historian and novelist with a special interest in the American Revolution. His research was conducted over thirty years during regular visits to the U.S. The author appears well versed in the common disrespect between Gen. Gates and Gen. Arnold.

In retrospect: Arnold's exploits at the surrender of Fort Ticonderoga, surrender of Fort St. John, coping with the extreme hardships on the march through the Main wilderness, the siege on Quebec which he maintained through the winter of '75/'76, his delaying and turning of Carleton's British army, his reaction to the raid on Danbury, his successful ruse to deplete the force of Lt. Col. St. Leger causing him to retreat from his siege on Fort Schuyler, when lacking authority his superior influence with army men in spurring them to defeat Burgoyne at Bemis Heights are individually either heroic or above and beyond the call of patriotic duty. Collectively they indicate that Arnold was a Super-patriot. Arnold was ambitious, impetuous, brave and a proven leader of man, all qualities that are desired in military officers. The root of the problem that repeatedly plagued Arnold was the fledgling Continental Congress.

1. Feb. '77, Congress *failed* to promote Arnold, instead promoting 5 who were junior in Arnold's rank.
2. After Arnold's response to the British raid on Danbury, Congress did promote Arnold but *failed* to restore his seniority.
3. Congress appointed the inept Horatio Gates to replace retiring General Schuyler.

"Common history paints glowing accounts of accomplishments by our "Founding Fathers", unfortunately reality has shown that nepotism and the "Buddy System" were working their ill effects even at that that time. Sad to say, the "Buddy System" and its potential for ill effects, remains with us today.

It is a shame that Arnold appears to have been driven to his traitorous course of action!

Benedict Arnold's greatest achievement in behalf of the patriots during the Revolutionary War occurred after Gen. Gates stripped him of authority, and of his own volition he joined the front line at the battle of Bemis Heights, where his very presence inspired the patriots to defeat Burgoyne's British army. The winning of that battle caused desired effects elsewhere. France and England had been at odds. Diplomat Ben Franklin succeeded in gaining France as an arms supplier, but had failed to convince France to join the patriots in their war. Judiciously France wanted evidence of a firm commitment by the patriots who as yet had not won a major battle. Consequently, the patriot victory at Bemis Heights, in large part due to the efforts of Arnold, convinced France to declare war on England and become a full-fledged ally of the patriots, supplying both army and navy. The navy of France was of the utmost importance because the patriot navy could not begin to compete with that of the British who had the capacity at will to blockade the patriot's ports. If France had not entered the war, the war's outcome would surely have been quite different and probably not to our liking.

Today we cannot celebrate Benedict Arnold as a hero of the war because he was *driven* to traitorous activity by the ineptitude of the continental congress and the ineptitude of the "buddy" of congress, General Horatio Gates.

When folks maltreat a dog long enough, then that dog will bite them back.

Bemis Heights is located only 25 miles from Schenectady where my ancestors were since Schenectady's beginning 1658-1662. With a sparse population, intermarriage with many early settlers was common. Lineal ancestor Arent Albertse Vedder served in the First Regiment of the Line under Col. Goosen Van Schaick. My lineal ancestot Albert A. Vedder served in the 2nd. Albany Co. Militia under Col. Abraham Wemple. Colaterals Johannes, Frans and Alexander served in the 2nd. Albany County militia as did another colateral Alexander together with his son Nicholaas. It seems most likely that they participated in the left wing at the battle of Freemans Farm under Benedict Arnold, and later participated in the battle of Bemis Heights. I wish I could question them about Arnold.

No doubt there were many among my early maternal ancestral lines that participated as well.

I could continue with this but only at risk of resorting to radical rant, so I will stop before that occurs.

A FEW MORE INCOMPETENTS THAT HAVE REARED THEIR UGLY HEADS IN AMERICA FROM TIME TO TIME

In the War of 1812, General William H. Winder proved incompetent at the battle of Stony Creek, losing to the British, even though his army was three times larger. In 1814 Winder commanded the forces protecting Washington, D.C. from the invading British. One charge by the British routed Winder's army, and he fled for safety. Subsequently the British sacked and burned the American Capitol.

During the Civil War's battle of Antietam, General Ambrose Burnside continuously ordered Union troops to cross a narrow bridge where they were exposed and served as sitting ducks for Confederate riflemen. If Burnside had investigated, he would have known that the creek below was at most waist deep and could have been easily forded by his troops thereby avoiding the bridge where so many Union troops were killed. My great-great aunt Nancy married Aaron Glazier and they lived in Minnesota. Aaron and two of their sons were killed at the battle of Antietam, said to be the bloodiest day of the Civil War with 22,000 confederates and 20,000 union troops killed.

At the 1865 siege of Petersburg, Burnside had a tunnel dug beneath the confederates trenches, and filled with explosives. The blast left a huge crater. Burnside ordered his troops into the crater where they were trapped and shot down by confederate along the crater's rim. President Lincoln subsequently remarked, "Only Burnside could have managed such a coup, wringing one last spectacular defeat from the jaws of victory".

During the Civil War, The Union's General McClellan on several occasions had General Lee at a disadvantage. If McClellan had immediately followed up at those times, the Civil War would no doubt have ended much sooner than it did.

General Ulysses S. Grant, a confirmed addict of caffeine, nicotine and booze seemingly functioned fairly well during the Civil War. Perhaps because he had a few good men under his command. Grant's incompetence was displayed during the terms he served as president, when more graft and scandal riddled the Federal government than at any other time.

Teddy Roosevelt, who falsely claimed his rough riders were the victors at San Jaun Hill. they did participate but it was at some other hill over yonder. Teddy also made irrational statements condemning Moyer and Haywood while they were in jail awaiting their trial. Eugene Debs was included in Teddy's badmouthing. Masses of working people retaliated by marching in protest.

Van Olinda; Philippus, bp. July 29, 1776. The following advertisement was published by the late Judge Sanders, Sen., in the *Albany Gazette:*

"On Thursday, the 4th instant, about four miles from the city of Schenectady, aside the Mohawk turnpike, sitting under a tree, I discovered Petrus Groot, who was supposed to have been slain in the Oriskena battle under General Herkimer on the 6th of August, in the year 1777. I immediately recognized him, and on conversation with him, he confessed himself to be the person I took him to be. I then carried him to the nearest tavern,* where I left him to be sent to his children and brothers, from whence, however, he departed before

---

* The house to which he was taken, was occupied by Simon Van Patten, better known as Cider Simon, from the circumstance of his manufacturing large quantities of cider annually. Van Patten identified him by a mark on his leg, occasioned by the bite of a rattlesnake, which he remembered from the circumstance of its having been cured by an Indian applying a leaf through which he sucked the poison with his mouth, leaving it perfectly free from soreness.

day the next morning, and was seen in Albany on Friday. His mental faculties are much impaired, supposed to have been occasioned by a wound of a tomahawk near the fore part of his head, though he is at most times tolerably rational. His head is bald; the circle or scar of the scalping knife is plainly to be seen on it, and a stab on the side of his neck near his shoulder; has a small scar near his ancle; is a middle sized man, has blue eyes, a long countenance, and stoops much in the shoulders. He speaks English, French, Dutch and Indian, and says he has been last a prisoner among the Indians north of Quebec; had on an old dark grey coat and old brownish pantaloons; has a large pack with him. He refused to go home, as one of his former neighbors whom he saw, would not recognize him, he was fearful his children and brothers would not. He said he would go to the governor's. Being at times deranged, it is feared he will stray too far away for his friends to find him. He is of a very respectable family and connexions. Any person who will take him up and bring him to the subscriber, at Schenectady, shall be well compensated for his care and trouble, and will receive the sincere thanks of his children and the relatives, and be the means of relieving this poor unfortunate man from distress by restoring him to his family and friends.

JOHN SANDERS.

SCHENECTADY, June 8, 1807.

N.B. The printers in this and the neighboring states are requested to give the above a few insertions in their respective papers, to aid in restoring a poor sufferer to his children and friends, who has been thirty years a prisoner among the Indians. He is now 63 years of age. He was a lieutenant in the militia at the time he was supposed to have been slain."

Originally from New England, Jonathan Pearson long served as professor of Natural History at Union College and maintained a lifetime hobby researching early settlers of that area. Some Four or five books resulted from his efforts, all published about 1875.

Pearson apparently found the attached in the archives of the Albany Gazette.

I found it personally interesting for the reason that Judge John Sanders, Petrus Groot and 'Cider" Simon Van Petten were all distant cousins of mine.

However, it is also interesting in that Groot was taken captive at Oriskany in what has been heralded as the bloodiest battle of the Revolutionary War. When the British planned a three prong attack to meet at Albany as to sever the New England Colonies from the others. British Col. St. Leger had laid siege to Fort Schuyler (formerly Fort Stanwix) And Gen. Herkimer had assembled 800 Mohawk Valley militiamen to march for the Forts relief. However Herkimer's force was ambushed at Oriskany not far from the Fort. Early on, Herkimer was badly wounded in a knee but he insisted on being placed seated on a fallen tree where he could observe the battle. Noticing that each time a militiaman fired, at least two Indians would rush and tomahawk him before he could reload his musket, Herkimer ordered his militiamen to fight in pairs, each reserving his firing until the other had reloaded. At dusk the Indians and tories retreated to their siege of the Fort, and for that reason the patriots considered it a victory, but having lost more than half their force as casualties the militia limped back to the Mohawk Valley. With the hot August weather, Herkimer's wounded leg suffered, and not many days following the amputation of his leg, he died.

General Benedict Arnold, with 1,000 men was dispatched from army headquarters near Albany for the purpose of relieving the siege of Fort Schuyler. Arnold effectively used a ruse, knowing that Indians were held in awe by non compo mentis folk (halfwits) he enlisted the aid of a non compo living in the Mohawk Valley who had a brother that was incarcerated, and by promising release of his brother, the halfwit agreed to take a message to St. Leger's force saying that Arnold was coming with a vast army, and believing the message, St. Leger's Indians deserted his force and the tories soon followed. With too few regulars to continue, St. Leger retreated to Canada. In this manner, Burgoyne was deprived of St. Leger's force at Saratoga. British Gen. Howe at N.Y. City took his army to quell a problem at Philadelphia instead of joining Burgoyne up the Hudson. In part, circumstances unforeseen by the British resulted in Burgoyne's defeat at Saratoga.

Another interesting aspect of Groot's tribulations is that in 1807, Washington Irving worked at a N.Y. City newspaper. Often heralded as "THE FATHER OF AMERICAN LITERATURE", Irving made his first trip up the Hudson about that time. Known as a borrower Irving is said to have used the character of a school teaching friend for Icabod Crane. Borrowed the character of a Van Alen girl that Irving himself was seeing and used it for the girl that Icabod was going to visit. Borrowed Knickerbocker as a pen name and there had been Knickerbockers around Albany since 1650. Borrowed my name for an Innkeeper who forecast weather by the manner in which he smoked his pipe. Borrowed the name Van Winkle, and it's certainly obvious that he borrowed Petrus Groot's near 30 year captivity as a basis for the long nap of Rip Van Winkle. He even borrowed Judge Sanders description of Groot "a long countenance and stoops much in the shoulders".

THE UNSUNG HERO

At Oriskany, one recruit,
Of Herkimer's, was Petrus Groot,
Whose will to win, so resolute,
His bravery, so absolute,
In manner that he'd execute,
Successful effort to dispute,
Ambush, St. Ledger'd institute,
That ambush rendered dissolute.

The ambushers would execute,
Retreat, that we can attribute,
To valor shown by Petrus Groot.

Groot's will to win was so acute,
He took up ambushers pursuit,
His comrades did not follow suit,
Groot, reloading after he'd shoot,
Was taken captive, 'long that route,
And thus was rendered destitute,
Near thirty years, we can compute.

Near thirty years, as tortured brute,
Petrus returned home, destitute,
Of reason, bearing scars acute,
Which witnesses would attribute,
That tomahawks had execute',
And scalping knife had institute'.

Oriskany ambush dispute,
Success was such, as to bear fruit,
For then, Gates needed not dilute,
Saratoga force that dispute',
Successfully, Burgoyne's pursuit,
Of divide and conquer repute.

And Gate's success did constitute,
Reason France entered our dispute,
Whose navys help, we attribute,
Success in war of revolute',

Chain of events that followed suit,
From valor shown by Petrus Groot,
Indicates his actions were 'root
Cause for success in our dispute,
At gaining of Liberty's fruit.

Humble Petrus gained no repute,
As war hero of Revolute',
But his long absence was the root,
Inspiration for long nap, cute,
Of Van Winkle, Irving would toot.

THE RIVER

When it's early or when it's late
The McKenzie at Heavens Gate
Has lovely sight that does impart
A strong medicine for the heart
And tune that plays where riffles roll
Provides sweet music for the soul
Aloft where the eagles abide
The rapids which the ducks do ride
All total to an awesome place
Where we can witness nature's grace

SMATHOGRAPHY

Some folk think others use some trick
For solving problems mathmetic
They have not mastered rules basic

Once rule's mastered, method will click
Providing momentum to flick
Out an answer pretty darn quick

Chief ingredient is logic
Applied skid grease to help one pick
An answer that's not anemic

Rely on nothing politic
Too often that's all rhetoric
And seldom true answer will wick

Remember numbers baliwick
Important where value you'd stick
That correct answer, you can kick

A common equasion says pi
Circles area, not deny
When one would merely multiply
        It times the radius when squared
        For then the area is shared
        With anyone who has so cared
Because square of diameter
Is equal to four times greater
Than what squared radius refer
        Then one fourth pi when multiplied
        Times the D squared, also decide
        Circle area, to provide

And since both pi and one fourth pi
Are ever constants to apply
It would be wise if one would try
      Committing both to memory
      For an advantage then would be
      One knowing immediately
All areas for circles done
When diameters equal one
one fourth pi is the answer spun

                                                      .7853981634

      And when 2 is diameter
      The area one may be sure
      Has answer of which pi would cure

                                              3.1415926536

RECIPE FOR HANKY PANK

Within confines of solitude
deeper than the ocean,

Mix one gal, whose curvy shape
results from nature's notion,

With one guy on whom such shapes,
work as the strongest potion,

Add bushels of joint respect
and mutual devotion,

One tender smooch as leavening,
sets this mix in motion.

BLOODLINES

When I am asked of my bloodlines
In truth I must answer the signs
   Which I'm aware in family
   Are common to man's history
Some bloodlines are norweigian
And some are of boheimian
    Some from German, Mohawk and Swiss
    Some from a Wickelow Irish miss
      Some Chickasaw and Cherokee
      Walloon and Dane, I have in me
Some Swede, some Belgian and some Scot
Some English, but it's not a lot
    And those which I have very much
    Are the bloodlines of Holland Dutch
      Those bloodlines that I have in me
      Are what I know from ancestry
But from knowledge that man has found
Are bloodlines that to some, astound
    Cro-magnon and Neanderthal
    Are likely ancestral to all
      Methinks Austrolopithecus
      Bloodlines are had by all of us
And when man came down from the tree
He left bloodlines for you and me
    But, there's limits to what we know
    Like when man, up the tree did go
      None-the-less asked of my bloodlines
      I certainly must answer HEINZ

Hooray, Hooray, the first of May
Is time when gals and guys obey
The urge of nature that's risque
And romp together in the hay

Even puppies have the same trait
To mingle as they swing and sway
Because that is ma nature's way
To celebrate on PINXTER day

Worst of all wrongs since time began
Are corrupt folk who plot and plan
The restrictions of can't for can
Which infringe on the rights of man
Such misdirected partisan
Plotting is such that we should ban

SONG OF THE WURKIN STYF

Wun wurkin styf, hoo synged a song,
Hee synged off kee and synged it long,
Knot ownlee did hee knot exsell,
Hee synged with tu mutch dessabell.

If wee lysind tu hys noysee toon,
Frum exployturs skeems, weed bee imyoon,
Cuzz hee synged of a better day,
With a collerz wurk for a dollerz pay.

Boss stopt hym then, in myd reefrane,
Tolled hym tu nevver syng agane,
Tolled hym tu kwench hys noysee tung,
Whence all them dessabellz wuz rung.

For, if the boss kood cylance hum,
More of the prawfitz boss kood skym,
By keepun wajiz varee low
For all the styfz, boss had in toe.

All wurkun styfz, shood take thare ku,
Tu lurn thare song and syng it, tu,
Tu syng it loud and syng it long,
That all mite no of boss's rong.

The more that styfz thare song du air,
The grater chanz for wajiz fair,
So, all the styfz, with sho and telz,
Shood fill the air with dessabellz !

OLD IRONYSIDES

The gale forces which abound
    Off Cape Arago surely found
    New Carissa's anchor unsound
Wind blew her through the shoals to beach
Along the north spits outer reach
Where pounding waves, her hull did breach.
    But, folks so feared each molecule,
    Of New Carissa's leaking fuel,
    They'd strive at length to overrule,
The plan which nature had designed,
In hopes a better plan they'd find,
To keep the leaking fuel confined.
    Often nature would countermand,
    The many efforts that were planned
    To keep the oil off the sand.
At last the tug, See Victory,
Suceeded pulling the bow free
And started towing it to sea.
    Nature blew up a huricane,
    With force so great in tow line strain
    That it could no longer maintain.
It parted, setting the bow free,
To blow aground at the Alsea
And spread some more oily debris.
    Once again, unified command,
    Pulled the bow section off the sand
    This time all went as was planned.
With long tow by Sea Victory,
Where bow was scuttled in the sea,
By torpedo, artillery.
    On north spit, the stern does remain
    With potential to entertain
    With views of shipwreck on the main.

this saga surely is not free,
Of mans self imposed irony,
For there are some who'd rather see,
        Another effort launched in turn,
        To remove New Carissa's stern,
        Depriving tourists chance to learn,
Of mother nature's awesosome ways,
Which on occaision she displays
By tragedies which she conveys.
        But, those in tourist industries
        See stern as monument to please
        That draws tourists to tragedies
Knowing that such tourist will tend
To visit Coos Bay or North Bend
Where ultimately, they will spend.
        Another irony that's plain,
        Is man has long struggled to gain
        All oil that he can obtain.
        Oil from plants and beasts of yore,
        Some thought to be from dinosaur
        Remains which the earth has in store,
For there are many things men do,
By using oily residue,
To gain the things which they pursue.
        But oil use they'd regulate
        When spread upon the sea of late,
        It's treated as contaminate,
For any birds who since have died,
The new Carissa's beaching tide
Are blamed on oil, far and wide.
        That is gravest of ironies,
        For Science's technologies'
        Have studied the birds pedigrees,
And think the bird's progenitors,
Were none other than dinosaurs'
That all birds had for ancestors.
Yet folk think bird's deadliest banes,

Are coping with the oily stains,
Of their great granddaddy's remains.

EEORE

Since the above story took place, the court has awarded damages to the State of Oregon from the ship's company, one hefty bundle of moolah, which our ass toot Governor has wee-weed away to have the stern section removed, so much for the tourist attraction.

CHECKS AND BALANCES

The founders of our great country,
Designed government carefully,
With checks and balances to free,
Us from the threat of tyranny.

Three branches, they'd initiate,
Judicial would adjudicate,
Contested law, as to translate,
That law's intent, to keep it strait.

Executive would execute,
Laws that congress would institute,
With veto power to dispute,
Laws deemed to have flawed attribute.

Legislative would legislate,
The laws enacted by the state,
By way of scrutiny, debate,
To disallow a tainted trait.

The citizen's vote would decide,
On executive to preside,
And upon congressmen to guide,
Laws worthy of the country wide.

But now, our government has strayed,
From outline that our founders bade,
Appointed agencies have laid,
Enactment of laws that are made,

And citizen votes lack the clout,
For voting those appointees out,
When errant laws, they bring about,
Denying balance, there's no doubt.

Sans check and balance, appointees,
Can enact any laws they please,
Most of which tend to put the squeeze,
Upon citizen's liberties,

Lacking means to effectively,
Respond to laws by appointee',
For citizens, is certainly,
Equivalent of tyranny.

It's certain, that of congress, we,
Need insist be lone assignee,
To enact law for our country,
to rectify this travesty.

And insist congress has reviewed,
Restrictive laws that have accrued,
For valid cause and aptitude,
Before they are as law, construed.

Then if congress, to large degree,
Fails responsibility,
Voters can vote accordingly,
In defence of their liberty.

INDENSITY

One day a Scotchman met a Jew,
An argument then did ensue,
Of which most frugal of the two.

They argued up and argued down,
Each seeking for himself renown,
And right to wear the frugal crown.

Just as a Dutchman wandered by,
the trio, all at once, espy,
A spot where there a penny lie.

Then, all together, each made haste,
By stooping quickly, from the waist,
To grasp the penny they'd not waste.

Alas, with force their heads enjoin',
the Scot and Jew were both disjoin',
Hard headed Dutchman got the coin.

When Scot and Jew had regained touch,
Their reputations all asmutch,
They both saluted "Tam cheap Dutch".

For sure it is, amongst the three,
To be crowned King Frugality,
The Dutchman used indensity !

ALL!

High on a hill, two bulls once met,
One frisky, young; one old and set',
And far below them, the bulls gazed,
At herds of heifers as they grazed.

So excited by what he viewed,
The young bull stuttered as he mooed,
"What do you say, we run down there,
And then we make love to a pair?"

For that, old bull expressed disdain,
As he'd then moo quite loud and plain,
"I'd much rather we'd walk, not run,
And then make love to ev'ry one!"

ON THE ONE HAND

Once all the fingers joined in league and formed a coalition,
To press charges against the thumb, each signed a deposition,
Claiming the thumb abused them without asking their permission.

When questioned on the charges, the thumb, by his own admission,
Said finger permits were not sought and what was his omission,
By reason that he'd expedite his duty, acquisition.

The judgement handed down following lengthy inquisition,
Acknowledged that the thumb should remain in full opposition,
To accomplish the duties that were place din his commission.

As to the fingers, judge denied all that they did petition,
Demanding that combined with thumb, they maintain grip tradition,
And when the thumb had work to do, they must offer submission.

VARIED INTERESTS

It's quite difficult to explain,
But, a marked difference is plain,
Of what intrigues folks 'bout each grain.

For rice that's of a wild strain,
It sure appears that folks are fain,
To address harvest, in the main.

Yet in the wild oat domain,
The interest which folks maintain,
Seems ever in the sowing vein.

Perhaps that's why, among the twain,
Wild oats wax, wild rice wane,
From interests folks entertain.

UNHEEDED WARNING??

Full century in 'ninty six,
Since its erection did affix,
Congress' Library's bailiwicks.

When artists of those days took part,
To decorate it's walls with art,
In themes which they chose to impart.

One lone artist chose government,
As the theme which he would present,
His five paintings are testament.

From central, "GOVERNMENT", right, read,
"GOOD ADMINISTRATION", that lead,
To "PEACE AND PROSPERITY", creed.

But, "CORRUPT LEGISLATION", left,
Displays a government that's cleft,
By avarice for bribes they'd heft.

Which naught but leads to "ANARCHY",
Where justice is full absentee,
And there's no sign of liberty !

Eliho Vedder chose the theme of government, and when another artist
failed to complete his commission, Vedder created a mosaic of Minerva
over 16 feet tall. Perhaps he is best known for his illustrations of the
Robaiyat for Hougheon-Mifflin

Throne of Dreams

During the years of yesteryore,
I'd assume challenges galore,
And seldom ever shirk a chore,

But, now when chores demand I jump,
I seek and find excuse to slump,
And comfy place to park my rump.

In practiced habit to ignore,
The challenges that went before,
Accumulating evermore.

For challenges, once high and plump,
Become inconsequential lump,
Once I am perched upon a stump.

'Cause then my plans and dreams can soar,
With challenges that I'd explore,
Which my mind's eye might have in store.

Devising thoughtful ways to trump,
All challenges my dreams can pump,
When on a log. I'm dreamy bump.

ON THE ONE HAND

All the fingers were dainty girls,
With blushing cheeks and locks of curls,
Who ranged in size from Pinkie, small,
Up to miss Mid, who was quite tall,
With Ring and Index sized between,
But none could be construed as lean,
For each possessed the full figure,
Of female who's quite mature.

The lone man in their neighborhood,
Mister Thumb, did all that he could,
To catch their eye to flirt and grin,
Obsessed with all things feminine,
For their attention, he would strive,
With his hormones in overdrive,
And e'er they strayed within his reach,
thumb ne'er failed to twiddle each.

Except Pinkie found she could run,
Faster than Thumb with fly undone,
For once he'd got her mittens down,
But Pinkie hiked hem of her gown,
And ran so fast from his embrace,
That Thumb, she'd easily outpace,
And after that, she'd never stray,
Within Thumb's reach, but stay away.

For twiddling thumb, she never would,
And thus preserved her maidenhood.
then only thoughts that crossed Thumb's mind,
Were thoughts of Pinkie's cute behind,

And all of his spare time was spent,
At plotting Pinkies ravishment.
Thumb's plots were to no avail,
Pinkie's shyness would prevail.

In plotting, Thumb would full ignore,
The fingers he had caught before,
Then loud were wails of Miss Ring,
Who sorely missed the Thumbs twiddling,
Miss Mid felt caught in the middle,
'Cause Thumb denied her a twiddle,
The plight similar for Index,
Who quite enjoyed a twiddling flex

For when they'd shimmy their behind,
No attention from thumb, they'd find,
And going topless was in vain,
That too, no attention would gain,
Or even dancing in the buff,
'Cause Thumb fully ignored such stuff,
E'en though they'd flaunt themselves about,
That trio had to do without.

Then each one of that trio mourned,
That by the Thumb, they had been scorned,
For no more twiddling was engaged,
By all that group, as on they aged,
So involved was Thumb's obsession,
To claim Pinkie, his possession.,
That all Thumb's masculinity,
Unused, began to atrophy.

Then after many years elapsed,
The Thumb's pink obsession collapsed,
And once again he'd offer chase,
To trio which now felt disgrace,
And feeling they'd been scorned before,
That trio would, the Thumb ignore.

So all Thumb's efforts were in vain,
For he was treated with disdain.

Ring resorted to the action,
Of practiced self satisfaction,
As similarly Miss Middle,
Often gave herself a twiddle,
And it was certain Miss Index,
Alone, engaged in pseudo sex.
Collectively, that trio sought,
That none, by Thumb, was ever got.

Rendered inactive in his need,
Thumb's ability atrophied,
Then often in his thoughts, he rued,
That too long, pinkie, he'd pursued,
And genuinely sorry for,
Those times, the trio he'd ignore,
But in the end, Thumb did admit,
His lust for Pinkie had caused it.

Over the years, Pinkie had hope,
That some young thumb, she'd meet to grope,
But that which she hoped would occur,
Had totally evaded her,
And she became fully afraid,
That she would end up an old maid,
A situation she'd avoid,
If with some thumb, she could have toyed.

Then Pinkie wondered deep in thought,
What might have been, had old Thumb caught,
Her years before, what taken place,
If the old Thumb had won that race,
Then realized her old maid lapse,
Was caused by her fast run, perhaps,

And she decided on that day,
That she'd now run opposite way.

All her misgivings, she'd erase,
As she commensed, old Thumb to chase,
And though she'd primp all of her pink,
She could not get old Thumb to think,
Thoughts that were amorous enough,
That he might hope to do his stuff,
So Pinkie also, was deprived,
Of gaining status which she'd strived.

The trio, Miss Pinkie and Thumb,
In their old age would each succumb,
From lonliness which each had caused,
Years before when they had not paused,
All options, to investigate,
Which effectively sealed their fate.
Some things early, we'd not adopt,
Are later, things we cannot opt!

    The moral of this story, true,
    Is that lovers will seldom do,
    The things which are preferred by you!

THE DIFFERENT DRUMMER

Often data available,
Is insufficient to gain full,
And apt conclusion, meaningful,
The following's an example.
        It happened that a child, young,
        Was oft' exposed to ditty sung,
        Whose single message of renown,
        Was London bridge is falling down.
Some years later, that same child,
Chanced to read Call of the Wild,
And learned that story had been spun,
By author who was named London.
By then, the child could not tell,
If story 'wrote before bridge fell,
Or if the bridge failing occurred,
Before that story had been heard.
        Still later, 'child was annoyed,
        On learning London's name was Lloyd,
        For memories from away back,
        Recalled that London's name was Jack.
        Child concluded, Lloyd, perchance,
        Jack used when selling insurance,
        Or perhaps Lloyd used the name Jack,
        Only when stories he would hack.
'Child survived teen age tumult,
To later become an adult,
And labored long, combatting strife,
That's associated with life,
Learning, when aged, one's problem is,
Coping with ills of rheumatiz,
Learning less suff'ring is endured,
By those refered to as snow bird'.
So the suffering adult planned,
To winter in a southern land,

110

But there, seeing London bridge spanned,
From supports that as yet do stand,
On scope of Arizona sand,
Was difficult to understand.
Surely that bridge, did never fall,
Had they been spoofed when they were small?
Was it a spoof, that Wild's Call,
Had been wrote by London, at all?
Was it a London spoof, perchance,
That Lloyd ever sold insurance?
And since such spoofing did occur,
How much spoofing did they incur?
How many tales fraught with flaws?
Perhaps there was no Santa Claus!
And perhaps spoofing rampantly,
Also applied to Tooth Fairy,
As well as the Easter Bunny!
Perhaps data, that a baby,
Comes via stork, was spoofery!
Since so much spoofery arose,
Perhaps that Pobble did have toes!
Perhaps Miss Mouse, that Froggie'd woo,
Was merely all spoofery, too!

> Then that adult would reminisce,
> Past occurrence of that or this,
> Which had lacked data evident,
> To gain conclusion sufficient.
> For it became quite obvious,
> Full data's needed to discuss,
> And apply ere conclusions spawn,
> From dataless deductions drawn.

Perhaps cause of ozone, holey,
Is something we cannot forsee,
Not from the Al Gore spoofery,
Of dataless rhetoric, he,
Has tried to foist on all of us,
With false conclusions, ominous!
Perhaps the conclusion that we,

Should try to coddle some specie,
Knowing that nature has resolve,
To ever press them to evolve,
In changing manner, where they've hope,
With ever changing earth, to cope,
May in the long run, prove to be,
Conclusion drawn on spoofery,
If for species, coddling denies,
Attained evolvement exercize,
Which nature ever full' applies,
For species to avoid demise.
If pampered species yet sucumb,
When forced to march by nature's drum,
We then will know, such spoof was dumb!
It's not that we have data lacked,
About how nature does impact,
All species failing to react,
Aptly to changes she'd enact.
Sans data to aptly compose,
A conclusion, nobody knows,
If mother nature will dispose,
Of pampered species in repose?
Likewise, sans data that disclose',
Apt answers to questions that pose,
What cause effectively arose,
That left the Pobble without toes?
On both questions, our legacy,
Marches to drums of spoofery!

STATESMANSHIP

So great at state was Pericles,
That rival Thucydides,
When writing in his histories,
Said naught but good in eulogies.

And mankind's first democracy,
Was all financed by currency,
In tribute from her colonie',
While citizens remained tax free.

today we have democraplot,
That taxcs citizcns a lot,
And spcnds much morc than wc havc got,
On endless lists of tommyrot.

And still the spending escalates,
While deficits are left to fates.
Electees promise more rebates,
While giving 'way all our estates.

To most this spending pill is tart,
And some have even lost all heart,
'Cause others yet, think it quite smart,
To owe the bank their nether part.

And men of state, we've none, no sir,
That can compare with ancient 'Per',
Our only recourse, I infer,
Is 'neath their tail, place a bur.

Then should they fail to go far,
Bring on the feathers and the tar,
That seems the only way to bar,
Them from the fiscal cookie jar.

And only way that I can see,
To make them stop the misery,
They now inflict on you and me,
And all of our posterity.

Vexing Verse of Vedder

UNIVERSAL SOLVENT

When we have toiled for some time
We get besmeared with grit and grime
Sometimes even spattered with slime
  And at those times, we've cause to think
  Of some method that's sure to link
  Us with removal of the stink
    And thus we become diligent
    In scrubbing up to large extent
    Using universal solvent
When that task we're undertaking
It is best if we're forsaking
Cold solvent, to keep from shaking
  For the solvent when it is warm
  Defeats shivers and does perform
  Far better results than the norm
    With warm solvent use our routine
    Coupled with a scrubbing we've seen
    An end result that's spiffy clean

We the residents of the greater metropolitan area of Parkersburg have formed a FOLKS FOR FREEDOM league which established a consensus to banish the blight of bureaucracy by eliminating the requirement of permits and licenses.

Spit and chewing gum
When folks finances are mere bit
They will use chewing gum and spit
To gain the things they hope to get
  Such ingredients opposite
  Must be reworked to make them fit
  Before they are of benefit
    And then their use knows no limit

For their usage will then permit
A host of projects infinite
No recipe exists in writ
So measures are not definite
For projects that we do submit
But when their use we do commit
With tongue in cheek we must admit
Results are not all exquisite
Yet for those folk who would omit
Indebtedness seen as befit
Are folk whom we respect their wit
They are the folk who have the grit
With ambition which they acquit
And are the folk who never quit

THE UNWIT'S WRIT

For the most part, contemporary writers of free verse fail to write with meaningful phrases so that much of their effort has remained in clouded ambiguity. Many have a penchant for using uncommon terms or terms in an uncommon manner, which is an attempt to gain some of the advantage that is enjoyed by metered rhyme. That is not to imply that we "trite and passe" writers of rhymed verse do not struggle for meaningful phrases in a continuous manner that explicitly relates an intended message that is easily understood. It's probable that metered rhyme helps attain that objective. The remarkable belligerence of free verse writers to avoid at all costs, the use of any terms which remotely suggest rhyming is reminiscent of the adage of "cutting off one's nose to spite their face". But then free versers are well conditioned in the area of spite.

Methinks haiku's lone saving grace
Is that it occupies less space
Than that which free verse does disgrace

SPUDS

Like Al Capp's schmoo, potatoes do
Provide for more than just a few
For breakfast they're tasty delight
When raw fried, taste is out of sight
And breakfast of some hash browned spud'
Is tasty and far from a dud
Mashed browned patties sure taste good too
No doubt taste better than a schmoo
With eggs and bacon on the side
They're preferred breakfasts far and wide
French fried potatoes served for lunch
Are tasty for all folk to munch
And tater salad hits the spot
For folk who do like it a lot
Also skinny potato chips
Are engineered to use with dips
When spuds for lunch, one does employ
Those are lunches that folk enjoy
For dinner many folks abide
For taters roasted in their hide
Adding butter or sour cream
Provides dinner that folks esteem
Scalloped potatoes fix a dish
As one which many folk would wish
Spuds that are boiled taste good too
And serve as base for veggie stew
Because of all that taters do
A common spud would shame a schmoo

AMAZONIA, DATELINE DAY
BEFORE YESTERYEAR

Phred Phunk, phactor oph phorphend phor phreckle phaced phrogs phounded phrom phhriends oph phoam phorest phound phumbling phigs phlouished phiphtyphold phrom phrothy phrog phlop. Phlourishing phigs phumbled phoam phorest phorever phorcing phlight oph phreckle phaced phrogs phrom phactor phunks phorphend.

POLITICIANS

Some think a politician high
      Opinion differing have I
            Too many I've seen cheat and lie
                  And basic rights they would deny
Too many of them only try
      To gain themselves a piece of pie
            Which never seems to satisfy
                  And does leave one to wonder why
Their actions only qualify
      As lame effort to justify
            That from us, our rights, they would pry
                  With restrictions they'd ratify
Veracity does not apply
      To those possessed with ilk so wry
            With ego that would glorify
                  And make attempt to dignify
In sinful manner that's quite sly
      They'd empty our tax fund supply
            Their supporters, to mollify
                  So as to retain their allie
Our lone hope is to rectify
      Their many ills that multiply
            With refusals, We'd not comply
                  With edicts that they'd certify

THE DOING OF CHEWING

Insufficient mastication
      OFTEN CAUSES CONSTIPATION
            With a belly ache duration
                  And potty preoccupation
Interfers with expectation
      For a normal conversation
            Or any cause for elation
                  With the planning for vacation
Far from being captivation
      It is total agravation
            With a dose of tribulation
                  Added to the pain sensation

NUMBERS

Numbers we use are arabic
Their common use arithmetic
Signed number use is reductic
And commonly called algebric
Joy of joys is geometric
Some is plane, some is spheric
There's analic geometric
That's always solved by algebric
Interesting is trigmetic
Some dealing with functionic
Rationic and proportionic
Both common and nat. logaric
And the pebble named calculic
The zero number arabic
Allows notation scienteic
To ease placing decimic
In problems of multiplic
As well as those dividic

CONCEIT, OR WHAT'S DID
BY BID OF THE ID

Folks say it is an ego trip
When all too oft' one's tongue does slip
Me's and I's in the thoughts they quip
      That's wrong! Such is trip of the Id
      Which superego has outdid
      Causing such terms of tongue amid
When me's and I's the tongue does bleat
The listeners quite often retreat
From recognizing such conceit
      Surely we all should recognize
      The language which we all despise
      Is freely laced with me's and I's
But language lacking all such muss
Is language using we's and us
Which we consider fabulous

COQUETRY

The coy campaign of a coquette
Can cause a guy to be beset
With primal urges that he'd get
      Because all guys possess the trait
      Of strong impulse to procreate
      And consequently seek a mate
It may very well be the aim
Of the coquette to gain the same
Using coyness to hide her game
Of the behavior as a vamp
To lure the guy into her camp
Where she can brand him with her stamp

STEPHEN KING

Integral to Steve King story
    Is a plot that's grim and gory
        A plot which he intends to steer
            The reader through substantial fear
Conditioning readers to dread
    The story which might lie ahead
        Knowing that spoon-fed travesty
          Spurs readers curiosity
All King's stories seem to frolic
    Steeped in substance diabolic
        Of every devilish, evil thing
         Of fearful writ, he is the KING

PEACE

The days of yore
      That went before
            The Norse god Thor
                  Waged hammer war
                        That left foes sore
                              In blood and gore
                                    We'd not adore

But we'd implore
      That Norse author
            Of thunder roar
                  To full 'explore
                        Joining Peace Corps
                              To quite score
                                    Of noisy lore

LIBERTY

The cornerstone of liberty
    Has been the rights of property
        Which maintains the stability
            Of all people who would be free
All legislated cant's the thing
    Which stops the bell of freedom's ring
        With resulting chaos to bring
            Cause for library to take wing
Seems we must make internal war
    To stop all of the can't before
        Our efforts fail to restore
            Our liberty forevermore

MY ERRANT SONG

Insinging my errant song
    I hesitate to tell
The many words that are sung wrong
    Are words that I sing well

———————————————————

ALL OF US !

When April one is drawing nigh
There is one thing we can't deny
As fools, we sure all qualify
    For people that would seek to pick
    Unwary souls that they might trick
    Between the ears, themselves are thick
        And after all is said and done
        In trickery on April one
        We question just which fool has won
            On April one, the All Fools date
            There's few indeed who contemplate
            'Tis we, ourselves, we celebrate

GREEN !

Stones of blarney and shamrock lawns
Shillelagh toting leprechauns
    A day for wearing of the green
    Sampling Emerald Isle poteen
        All circumstanced, which happens that
        In reverence of good Saint Pat
            From Wickelowe to Galway Bay
            A day when elves and fairies play

ESTEEMED TITLE

As through life's years, we slow' ascend
    We learn from those whom we depend
        The greatest tribute in the end
        Is when we are addressed as friend

Best I Ken !

I'm doin' very best I ken
    To 'spress myself with pointy pen
        'Cause from my thick, unwieldy tongue
        All decibels are off-key rung

SALTY !

It ain't the blue pacific breeze
      That makes my brain so faulty
            It slips a cog when e'er I sneeze
            And then my thoughts get salty

Fokes iz dumm whar I kum frum
      Wee eint hed eny larnin
            Stil weir happee az kin bee
                Duin whut kumz natcherlee

FADING IN THE NIGHT

In autumn when the leaves are fall'
Spooks and goblins bedevil all
Ghosts and witches pay us a call
Ringing doorbells at every hall
      With implied tricks, they then coerce
      Sweetmeats in tribute for their purse
      And woe to those who don't imburse
      Trickery then is intersperce'
            But folk who pay their due in fright
            Are never vexed with such a plight
            For witch and goblin, spook and sprite
            Will then go fading in the night

X-RATED

'Appears that in pre-history
The ratings were no mystery
'Cause those who dwelled in caves on cliffs
Have left x-rated hieroglyphs
    And, sure as sin, 'tis that Astarte
    'Twas one that played x-rated part
    While others wrote about more sex
    In undeciphered linear x
        The Mongols carried many skirts
        On horseback to their pagan yurts
        While Druids sang their bawdy tunes
        All written in x-rated runes
            Bundling was once x-rated mode
            At the New Englanders abode'
            While Indian lad and lass agree
            'tis fun to often play tepee
                X-ratings are a means, 'tis sure
                For censoring our thoughts impure
                We've cause to think, our futures fate
                Will include thoughts and deeds x-rate'
                We yet express x-rated sign
                Bequeathed us by Saint Valentine
                'Cause thoughts impure are oft' display'
                On our x-rated holiday

TWITTERPATION

Ssure 'nuff, those struck by Cupid's dart
All suffer similar the fate
Within the head, about the heart
In symptoms of the twitterpate
On another, they then focus
    Their attentive twitterpation
    Manifest by hocus pokus
    Singing of their hearts elation
        Valentines of February
        Oftentimes, provide a clue
        That someone is plotting merry
        Twitterpation, because of you
Methinks Mohammed's catechism
Has spawned all the fanaticism
And all the BAD
Causing Jihad
Which results in terrorism

GOIN' GUNNY-BAG

When little time for us remains
We've plugged up arteries and veins
With blood pressure showing red flag
When we are goin' gunny bag

For then it seems to be our lot
To become a barrel of snot
On which we ever hack and gag
When we are goin' gunny bag

Then when we go tout and about
With our sciatica and gout
All of our movement does but lag
When we are goin' gunny bag

And when our mind thinks amorous
Results are naught but fret and fuss
As ED causes us to sag
When we are goin' gunny bag

Small is the tolerance we bear
For taxes that are deemed our share
When a tax specialist does nag
As we are goin' gunny bag

And when we find the instructions
Are quite vague about deductions
The result is mind boggling drag
When we are goin' gunny bag

We've prescriptions for poison pills
Which vastly inflate our med bills
When we are faced with their price tag
As we are goin' gunny bag

When we experience pains and pangs
In double-darns and gross gol-dangs
Such does confirm we've hit a snag
And we are goin' gunny bag

When Hamm's Special Light does beckon
And we're thirsty, then I reckon
Just two beers puts us on a jag
As we are goin 'gunny bag

And then it comes as no surprise
That those tow beers affect our eyes
And we will ogle any hag
When we are goin' gunny bag

LULLABIES

Perhaps the most common:

Rocr-a-bye baby in the tree top
When the wind blows the cradle will rock
When the bough breaks the cradle will fall
Down will come baby, cradle and all

Pray tell, why does a lullaby put a baby
at such risk?

Lullaby by Samuel Hoffenstein

Sleep, my little baby, sleep;
You'll have cause enough to weep-
Slumber is a precious boon;
You'll be getting measles soon;
Mumps will claim you for their own;
Croup will change your infant tone.
    Sleep, my little darling, sleep,
    Ere your first bicuspids peep
    Through your rosy little gums,
    And the envious colic comes.
Oh, the troubles time will ladle
On your happy baby cradle
Very shortly from the deep!-
    So, be wise, my lamb, and sleep.
More travesty to foist on a baby!!

Circa 1650 at New Netherland

Trip a trop a tronjes,   Take a short trip to dreamland

De varken in de boonjes,   The hogs in the bushes

De koejes in de klaver,   The cows in the clover

De paaden in de haver,   The pigs in the peas

De eenjes in de water plas,   The ducks in the puddle

De kalver in de l ang gras,   The calves in the long gra

So groot myn klein poppetje was.   So good my sweet darling i

The sensible Dutch were sensitive enough to not put a baby at risk in a lullaby.

WHAT'S THE BEEF?

Our forebearers numbers increase fast,
Through generations in the past.
So many did we have, indeed,
They represent all colors, creed'.

For one today, who thinks that we,
Have bloodline pure, has thought falsely.
Most every possibility,
Occurred within our ancestry.

We've each our share of victims, rogues,
At pyramids and synagogues.
Some represent the ill men do,
At Marathan and Waterloo.

By Golden Horde and by Crusade,
We've many, have to rest been laid.
'Tis sure all ancient history,
Now represents our ancestry.

So, those of us, who seek to paint,
their bloodline 'pure', without a taint,
From 'others', whom they've some complaint,
With ancestry, their not acquaint'.

For we're all brothers, near akin,
In spite of color of the skin,
In spite of custom or belief.
So, bigots tell me, what's the beef?

THE COLOR PURPLE

The color best for dress, I wot,
Is tiny yellow polka dot,
For ladies that would be demure !

And for a hat, worn fro and back,
the color best is blackest black,
to hold her straying tresses sure !

Red's best for roses, I would say,
And purple's best for corset stay,
Or dress for gals with thoughts impure !

THE UNSUNG DEITY

One thing we learn, soon after birth,
Time's of the essence, here on Earth,
With time to cry and time for mirth.

A time to rise from depths below,
A time to learn, a time to grow,
A time to practice what we know.

When all life's rivers, we have swum,
And naught remains, but to succumb,
It then is said, our time has come.

'Twould seem that Father Time should be,
The first and foremost deity,
Regarding immortality.

THE INTEGRAL PART

Ironic, when the press suppress,
The manner others do express,
While hooting loudly, none the less,
To maintain freedom of the press !

Rules of suppression that restrict,
Within themselves, are contradict',
All presses freedom is afflict',
By efforts made to interdict !

Suppressing tongues? Best for M.D. !
Speech freedoms best for you and me,
And few there are t'would disagree,
Integral part of liberty !

BASHFUL BILL

When yule assign,
Folk from the pine,
Would all combine,
with kith and kine.
    Then Flo would go,
    To stand below,
    The mistletoe,
    To smooch bestow.
        Her pap would run,
        To get his gun,
        In case someone,
        Had too much fun.
            And Bill would turn,
            All his concern,
            For buckshot burn,
            To quick' adjourn !
                Gus came from mine,
                To neighbors, jine,
                to dance and dine,
                And nip some shine.
                    Then Flo would show,
                    Her eyes aglow,
                    For want of beau,
                    And a trousseau.
                        Her pap would cuss,
                        And then he'd fuss,
                        His blunderbuss,
                        That Flo not muss.
                            Then Bill discern',
                          His tummy'd churn,
                          And all his yearn,
                          Was quickly spurn'.

Then Gus incline',
His jug of shine,
that tastes so fine,
Pap'd not decline.
    And pap would jus',
    Suck jug of Gus',
    To emptiness,
    Then sleep he mus'.
        When eyes of Flo,
        Saw pap'd not know,
        If oats she'd sow,
        To Bill, she'd go.
            When Bill discern',
            How Flo was yearn',
            He'd not return,
            To lone sojourn !

ONE A DAY

'Tis thought that every M.D.,
Might be reduced to poverty
If, daily, folks across the land,
Would eat one apple out of hand.

In doing so, folks might rejoice,
Of apples, we've near endless choice,
Available from sea to sea,
Of many a variety.

Most favor the Delicious, Red,
With flavor that but few might dread,
While Winesap's taste a bit unique,
In flavor others often seek.

While other's preferences, by gosh,
Are for the King, or McIntosh,
Yet those liking flavor mellow,
Often seek Delicious, Yellow.

And Baldwin, Lodi, Granny Smith,
Are still more types that folks do with,
Yet Glory Monday, dry and tart,
Provide a flavor quite apart.

Ben Davis does indeed festoon,
It's users with the shade, maroon,
Others yellow and many red,
Yet others remain green instead.

Russets too, in color tawny,
Some are small, while some are brawny.
Several types, mere piquant dabs,
All commonly, are known as Crabs.

Transparents mature quite early,
Jonathans grow big and burly,
Most preferred type, used in cuisine,
Remains the juicy Gravenstein.

Folklore claims we might stay healthy,
On daily diet of a Wealthy,
Or any other apple type,
But most are best when they are ripe.

More types for folks to choose from yet,
With which, their appetite to whet,
Alas, I cannot name them all,
There are too many to recall.

Some indulge in Apple Strudels,
Others stir-fry with their noodles,
One could easy, write a ballad,
Singing praise of Apple Salad.

Some pastries, cookies, pie and cake,
Require apple types to make.
Cooks are known to be quite handy,
Even making Apple Candy.

Jellies, Jams and Preserves are made,
With types of apples as an aid,
Or Juice, or Cider, Apple Jack,
Or out of hand, to munch a snack.

Some types are excellent for pie,
While sauce of some might please the eye,
And sure there's few that take affront,
With recipe for Apple Grunt.

Not long ago, the Alar scare,
Caused many orchardists despair,
But since the truth emerged again,
Those falsehoods have to rest, been lain.

"Cause orchardists just use Alar,
To chase the hungry bugs afar,
For people, no presage of doom,
'Less tons of Alar they consume.

The apple opportunity,
Bequeathed to us in legacy,
Providing in our time of need,
The fruits from Johnny Appleseed.
POA TREE

Sure, near and far, folks all agree,
That short and full, or tall and free,
The evergreen's a lovely tree.

Compared to other plants to mean,
This tree has always reigned as queen,
And earns our admiration, keen.

Methinks a rhyme shall ne'er be seen,
In merit, beauty, stature, sheen,
Compared to trees of evergreen.

Unless some green thumbed chap, by gee,
Can hybridize a Poa tree,
To grow those Poas for you and me.

So, if that chap can work his will,
On root and stem and chlorophyll,
All folks will hear those poas trill.

WILY WOMEN

My pappy told me, long ago,
"Beware those wily women,
'Cause if you don't, afore you know,
They'll have your head a swimmin',
You'd best say no to candleglow,
When dinner plates a brimmin',
And stop your senses to and fro,
When she goes off a primmin',
They like to turn the music low,
And keep the lights a dimmin',
'Cause then she's apt to smooch bestow,
Her arms, your neck a rimmin',
Then, if she wants you for a beau,
She may just start untrimmin',
And she'll have much to tell and show,
To keep your eyes a glimmin',
But, she'll say no of grass to mow,
When oats to sow, you're whimmin',
She'll have you know, that takes trousseau,
With all the chorus a hymnin' !"

OVERFLOWING GRAIL?

One wonders what had happened then,
Had Art been more attent' of Gwen.
Had Gwen yet strayed to other men,
Or faithful to her mate had been?

Or were Gwen's passion fires so strong,
That when ignored by Art for long,
She'd naught resist of Lance's song,
And thus commit to Art such wrong?

For Gwen in all her elegance,
Sure seemed to seize at every chance,
To be alone and meet with Lance.
Sure surely must have had hot pants !

Sir Lancelot, of knights, the best,
Would fail full' in moral test,
When passion pushed him to the quest,
Of meeting Gwen in ardent gest.

And so we learn from 'ancient tale,
Of Lancelot's flaws, and Art's travail,
Yet some answers are not avail'.
Was Gwen but Lance's holy grail?

TO THE OUTHOUSE

With tummy rumbling, here I sit,
Where crazies in conniption fit,
Have sometime lately, sat before,
And wrote in verse upon the door,
Most in vernacular uncouth,
On topics straying far from truth.
By straining, I soon hope to end,
My mission here, so I can fend,
These reeking odors from my nose,
And rush to sniff some fragrant rose!

DEAR GRANDDAUGHTER;

Today, most gals compete in haste,
To see who, first becomes unchaste.
Peer pressure now, for every maid,
That doesn't hasten to be laid,
With maidenhood's once revered gleam,
Now held in very low esteem.

While some still hold, 'tis only good,
To sit upon one's maidenhood,
And venture looks filled with disdain,
Toward any miss, who thus has lain,
Forgetting, they who cast first stone,
Should first clean-up acts of their own.

I'd hope that you don't spend your bod,
For thrills, just 'cause friends so it's mod,
Nor save yourself to just agree,
With those who flaunt their bigotry,
But you must judge, when time is nigh,
To share your love with special guy.

Then you'll rejoice, that you'd refrain',
From peer advice and bigots vain,
So you, yourself, earns YOUR respect,
In matters thusly circumspect.
Some cherished things are best to keep,
'Til great rewards, for us, they reap!

Love,
Gramps

AIN'T

We struggle when we've messages we'd pen,
To find a term that rhyme and meter fit,
That will not detract from our message when,
It is aligned with other terms we've writ'.

For always, the term which seems to fit best,
Fails in meter and also in rhyme,
And when one is found that with rhyme is blessed,
It fails meter and destroys the time'.

Our quest for terms that ever complement,
That meter, message flow and rhyme abet,
Too often suffers when we're negligent,
In finding terms that ain't invented yet!

THE GAME OF LIFE

Few things in life so well compare
As life itself with solitaire
In life we seek to 'fill our cup'
And littles changed in seven up
The game begins with little known
For there are only seven shown

That each Kings goal primarily
Is finding vacant property
And just as lifes laws say its sin
Hes not allowed to wed his kin

Just as in our lives we've seen
Fair Kings prefer a dusky Queen
While Kings sprung of a darker lot
Want Queens without a smutchy spot

Red or black, its each Queens goal
To suffer not from birth control
For often in a game we see
A family swelled with progeny

The man, the wife, the children too
All alternate by rule of hue
First children whether red or black
Are always first born sons named Jack
They after orderly produce
Their issue down from Jack to Deuce

Aces are victims of still birth
And go to heaven instead of Earth
Where once established, they are sure
To other younger children lure

All Queens and married Kings may opt
From groups of orphans to adopt
Sometimes, as life has often dread
A mothering Queen remains unwed
Her shame for eons, on and on
'less she's been visited by a swan'

And so in solitaire we see
This semblance of a family
And as in life, when game is done
We've cause to celebrate when won

But often though we try in vain
Some cards within our hand remain
For as in life, its left to fate
As when our game is terminate

Although its solitaire by name
All lifes reflected by the game
As well the game of life we bear
Is paralleled by solitaire

THE TIMELY DIET

It seems we seldom have the time,
To do the things we wish to do,
Because of clocks incessant chime,
Reminding us that time has flew.

So often tasks go unfulfilled,
As we are always running late,
And bleak, the habits we've instilled,
Conditioned to procrastinate.

For we are prone to take our ease,
As obligations multiply,
Some pray for time from deities,
They hope to gain from places high.

But, only Father Time has come,
To gobble each millenie, yum !

ANCESTORS

Our forebearers numbered in the pack,
Some thirty generations back,
Exceed earth's population !

How circumstances happened thus,
For every last one of us.
Mind boggling implication !

And not until we realize,
That many of those gals and guys,
Filled roles in duplication,

Can we e'er hope to understand,
That few were many, by demand.
Enlightening sensation !

And as we go back farther still,
The numbers will decrease until,
There's few in occupation.

We finally reach that point sublime,
When there's but ONE upon a time,
Referred to as creation !

And few there are that would agree,
Whether that ONE was he or she.
Much heated conversation !

Of Eve, there's some who think that she,
Was Adam's ribodectomy.
Macho preoccupation !

Sure there are those who might believe,
That Adam was mere rib of Eve.
A novel revelation!

Like chicken or egg being first,
Their arguments won't be reversed.
'Til all mere speculation !

BEGAT BEGUINE

It happened once upon a time,
When pristine Earth was yet sublime,
With mankind new, lust young and frosh,
Began Beguine began, b'gosh !

E'er since the human has been wrought,
They often dwell on impure thought.
That's why the earth today is fraught,
With many humans, thus begot.

Recipe for reproduction,
Webster labels as seduction,
Yet others say a lad and lass,
In spring are wont to mow the grass.

Humbly, here is my opinion,
term that's best for this dominion,
Neither Webster's nor mowing green,
But rather the Began Beguine !

BOWLS!

Science of archaeology,
Says mankind in pre-history,
Used first a bowl of hollowed stone,
As tool for purpose of his own.

And later learned to mold wet clay,
Then fire it for use, they say,
'Cause bowls are sure a needed tool,
For men to eat their bowl of gruel.

And bowls are good for porridge, too,
Or curds and whey, or mountain dew,
'Cause drunkards beg for bowl of grog,
To keep their senses in a fog.

When bowl evolved to lavabo,
Man learned to wash his hands, just so.
Learning that washing does not hurt,
Man devised games to play in dirt.

And that is how man came to play,
The football bowls on New Years Day !

WHEN ALL ELSE FAILS !

Surely we've all, each had some day,
When nothing seemed to go our way,
No matter what we'd do or say,
Each circumstance seemed to betray,
Us to an endless list of fray',
Ultimately, to our dismay,
Our outlook painted deep, dark gray.

And on those days, when thus assailed,
Trying much, and all has failed,
To render cause for such unveiled,
Or gain a clue of whence it hailed,
Our efforts subsequently paled,
By further events that prevailed,
And all of them were full travailed.

'Tis then that we, ourselves we doubt,
And self esteem suffers a drought,
When sanctuary or redoubt,
Cannot be found around, about,
While yet assailed from without,
By forces which we're constant clout',
Our only recourse then, to pout !

POUND OF FLESH

Our history says that folks of yore,
Oft' suffered times we might deplore,
From lack of things that we adore !

In times of famine, Turk and Greek,
And others struggled just to eke,
A sustenance that we'd deem bleak !

And in their struggle, some were fain,
To wrest what others had attain',
With usury their means to gain !

This antonym for charity,
With all its impropriety,
Is yet today in practice free !

And daily now, we see afresh,
The loan-sharks efforts, to enmesh,
Unwary souls for pound of flesh !

RESPECT!!!

'Twould seem we frequent' hear today,
Of Educations failed way',
And often folks will venture guess,
On what is need', to right the mess.

'Cause I like guessing, like a fool,
Here's my guess to improve our school'.
Pay young adults respect they're due,
They cherish it, like me and you.

How frequently we hear the phrase,
Spoken about our young these days,
When in a group, we are amid,
And someone says "They're only kid'".

"ONLY" is derogatory!
The young react ! Same old Story !
Common respect, we all adore,
When given youth, would change that score.

But "ONLY" is not the lone rogue,
Spoke by elder or pedagogue,
'Cause title "KID" can sure demean,
All young adults about the scene.

So, best we call them young adults,
With due respect. Improved results !
Yet, one step further, if I might,
We should respect their common right'.

Their common right to pick and choose,
If others rights they don't abuse.
Should elders this advice employ,
For every girl, for every boy,

Youthful reaction would be nip',
With vast' improved Deport-manship.
Reaction time might be devote',
To tangibles of scholar rote !

Sure seems to me, it's worth a try,
Before our learning well runs dry,
That Education, yet have hope,
To 'chieve the goals, for which we grope,

WITHIN

Sure each of us would like to quell
The beast that doth within us dwell
And never show our darker side
That each of us are "Mr. Hyde"
And keep our temper under rein
That we might always function sane.
Our trait that becomes manifest
Is inclination for conquest
In wars with others, we must best
Or competitions we contest.
Deep within our subconscious murk
Is where the beast's most apt to lurk
And where he's best retained in check
That rationality not wreck.
Best we remember, we all hath
Within, a smidge of phycopath.
For each of us a life long quest
To hide this shame, as can we best
But deep inside we understan'
That this condition is human!

UNKNOWN

Jane Doe was an enigma and she felt of little worth
Never learning circumstances that prevailed at her birth
Never learning of her mother, or her father, or her kin
Grappling always with the question of just what may have been
When her signature required, shes reminded of her cost
Caused by the unsolved mystery of her heritage thats lost
Throughout life she sought the answer to that question all in vain
An obsession with her history which brought her naught but pain
Having struggled with the problem, at lifes end she seeks relief
For she perceives in death an ally that might terminate her grief
Her problem is perplexing, for had we been 'thrown that bone'
Should we have fared as well as Janie, with a legacy unknown?

SWEETHEART BERRY

The Cranberry, so red and tart,
With flavor that is quite apart,
The other fruits in mans cuisine,
For sauce, remains our berry Queen.

Yet, sauce is not the only part,
For use their flavor does impart,
Cranberry juice with ruby sheen,
Provides a flavor, fresh and clean.

Their use in pastry is an art,
That tempts the tasters eye and heart,
With glory for the tongue, who mean,
To pass a taste, their lips between.

In breads and cakes, there's some who chart,
Cranberry use, that proves quite smart,
Because the folks, who thus would lean,
Partake of flavor unforeseen.

These ruby berries, from vines green,
Flourishing in dyked ravine',
With flavor that gives taste a start,
Provide us all, a Berry Sweetheart !

ONLY ONE

At Bandon, Oregon, County Coos,
We've many berries 'which to choose.
Youngs, Elders, Oregon Grapes folks use,
And Blacks and Rasps among the Dews,
Currants, Black Caps and Salmon ooze,
Salals and Straws along with Goose,
Thimbles and Hucks as well as Blues,
But, avoid Chittum berry stews,
And beward Deadly Nightshade, rues!

Still, when it's flavor we'd peruse,
There is but one we can't refuse,
And that is the CRANBERRY, whose,
Robust flavor must be diffuse',
In some fashion or by some ruse,
Or else one's tongue, one does abuse!
But, that same tartness does infuse,
Recipes with good flavor news,
Also, their varied scarlet hues,
In recipes, serve to amuse,
In different ways, with scarlet clues.

Vexing Verse of Vedder

Dear GTE;

Please know the access, I'd deplore,
Is smoke signal or semaphore.
All parties, whose access I seek,
Are those with whom I wish to speak.

And know that when I'm calling East,
I want the access that costs least,
And when I dial South or North,
I want no extra bucks put forth.

And should a call of mine go West,
At lowest price, I want the best.
Too tight to pay the awesome fee,
I call afar unfrequently.

Sure, I'd call more if it were free,
And that is my priority,
To be hooked to a free access,
Or barring that, one costing less.

The access I'd like best, I state,
Would refund double by rebate,
And should such refund escalate,
I promise, I'd accept that fate.

By now I'd hope that you can see,
I'm governed by frugality.
For me. I wish you'd access choose,
With cost so low, I can't refuse!

Frugally Yours
Leonard Vedder
Rt. 2, Box 570
Bandon, Oregon, 97411
503 347 3224

17 August 1994

Coos County Planning Department
Coos County Courthouse Annex
290 North Central
Coquille, Oregon 97423

Inre: Title of tax lot # 500; NW 1/4 of NW 1/4 of Section 27,
Twns.28, R. 14

I see no moral right that I,
Should decide for the other guy,
When neighbors wish to sell or buy,
Regardless of what you imply.

And furthermore, to clear the air,
My neighbors have no right to share,
Decisions made about my lair.
That right is solely my affair.

Yet on your planning map, I see,
You've taken 'way my property,
And given it away for free,
At sometime unbeknownst to me.

Does Babbitt know that you compete,
With usurpations, he'd complete,
By grasping titles by deceit,
To private property, delete?

I cannot help but wonder why,
My title, you would vilify,
Unless I failed to comply,
With some rare species edict, wry.

Yet species here are all well done,
Of rare types, I'm the only one.
But rights for being rare, I've none,
As ecosystem webs are spun.

170

So hopefully, I can rely,
Upon you for the reason why,
My title went to other guy,
And I await for your reply.

Leonard Vedder
Rt. 2, Box 570
Bandon, Oregon, 97411

PS I'd hope that you'd not think me rude,
But if my title, you'd exclude,
Your master plan sure should include,
The taxing of the other dude!

CC: Mr. Jackson, Coos County Assessor, Coos County Commissioners

THE CORDWAINER

In eighteen fiftynine, they say,
Mike Breuer first saw light of day,
In country, capital at Wien,
Apprenticed at age of thirteen,
Mike early learned shoemaking art.
When army drafted, he'd depart,
His homeland to gain a new start.

Thus, eighteen eightyone, they say,
Mike migrated to U.S.A.,
Where, a year later, it is said,
That Mike and Josephine were wed,
With four sons, three daughters, were blest.
They, eighteen eightysix, came west,
A middle fork homestead, to wrest.

In eighteen ninetyfour, they'd drop,
To Bandon, opening 'shoe shop,
A business that in time would grow,
With general merchandise to show.
Jo passed away in thirty two.
Aged ninety three, as cobblers do,
Mike mended shoes in fifty two.

Mike's shoe shop, built in ninety four,
Is building, Bandon's longest wore,
Surviving fire and hurricane,
Mike's shop devoted to cordwain',

Remains standing as testament,
To perseverance, sans relent,
Deserving full acknowledgement!

BEASTS OF BANDON

Here on the southern Oregon coast,
We've unique beasts, on which to boast,
Hard to distinguish, 'cause for most,
They blend within the common host.

Unlike Sasquatch, their feet are small,
Conditioned to a soft foot fall,
Which leaves no trace and thus forestall',
That ever they be tracked at all.

To ever see one on display,
One must arise 'fore break of day,
And brave the Oregon dewy spray,
To seek them out in just this way.

Seclude yourself in bushy spot,
Beside a boggy, berry plot,
That's where you'll see them, like as not,
Cause that's where they most often trot.

THANK THE LORD!

We know that Bandon gained its name from an Irishman named George,
Who sought respect from town folk with Lord title that he had forge',
His forgerys been recognized and he's denied much respect,
And he never would have came here, had the Lincoln never wrecked,
With Henry Baldwin counted from that shipwreck as surviving,
An early friend of George, he was the cause of George arriving,
And so when for causing Bandon's name, we seek someone to thank,
We might well consider Baldwin, with respect due for Lord Hank.